A FORMCRITICAL STUDY OF
SELECTED ODES OF SOLOMON

HARVARD SEMITIC MUSEUM

HARVARD SEMITIC MONOGRAPHS

edited by
Frank Moore Cross

Number 36
A FORMCRITICAL STUDY OF
SELECTED ODES OF SOLOMON
by
Gerald R. Blaszczak

Gerald R. Blaszczak

A FORMCRITICAL STUDY OF SELECTED ODES OF SOLOMON

Scholars Press
Atlanta, Georgia

A FORMCRITICAL STUDY OF SELECTED ODES OF SOLOMON

Gerald R. Blaszczak

©1985
The President and Fellows of Harvard College

Library of Congress Cataloging in Publication Data

Blaszczak, Gerald R.
  A formcritical study of selected Odes of Solomon.

  (Harvard Semitic monographs ; no. 36)
  Bibliography: p.
  1. Odes of Solomon—Criticism, Form.   I. Title.
II. Series.
BS1830.073B42   1985   229'.912   85-14345
ISBN 0-89130-917-9 (alk. paper)

Printed in the United States of America
on acid-free paper

To My Parents

ACKNOWLEDGEMENTS

I wish to acknowledge publicly at least some of the many people who made the present work possible. I am grateful to the Danforth Foundation whose fellowship grants helped finance my graduate school education. My brother Jesuits in New York, Cambridge and Jerusalem provided me with the material and moral support I needed during long years of research and study. If there is some scholarly merit in the present work, substantial credit belongs to the men who have been my teachers and mentors, especially Joseph Fitzmyer, S.J., Dieter Georgi, Helmut Koester and George MacRae, S.J. I owe a special debt of gratitude to John Strugnell, my dissertation director, who generously shared with me his time and his erudition.

I thank Frank Moore Cross for the honour of accepting this work for publication in the Harvard Semitic Monograph Series. I thank Joyce Bell for her patience and care in the typing and preparation of the manuscript of this work.

Gerald R. Blaszczak, S.J.

CONTENTS

CHAPTER I

Introduction

The history of scholarship of the Odes of Solomon begins
in the year 1785. In that year the British Museum purchased
the Codex Askewianus, a Coptic manuscript of the second half
of the fourth century, which came to be known as the Pistis
Sophia. In chapters 58, 59, 65, 69, and 71 the text preserves
several Odes ascribed to Solomon: Odes 1, 5.1-11, 6.8-18, 22,
and 25, according to the enumeration and versification proposed by R. Harris and A. Mingana.[1] Before 1785 the only
evidence for the existence of the Odes was the mention in the
sixth century Synopsis Sanctae Scripturae and in the sticho-
metry of Nicephorus (ninth century) of psalmai kai ōdai
Solomōntos, and a quotation in Lactantius, De Div Inst 4.12:

> Solomon in Ode undevicesima ita dicit: Infirmatus
> est uterus virginis et accepit foetum et gravata
> est, et facta est in multa miseratione mater virgo.

In 1909 J. R. Harris discovered that a sixteenth century
Syriac manuscript psalter from Mesopotamia contained poems
corresponding to those in the Pistis Sophia and to the verses
quoted in Lactantius. Odes 3-42, as they are numbered in the
Harris-Mingana edition, were contained in the manuscript.
Three years later F. C. Burkitt found a tenth century Syrian
manuscript containing Odes 17.7-42.20. Finally in 1959 M.
Testuz published the third century Bodmer Papyrus 11 which
contained Ode 11 in Greek.

From the time of their publication up to the present, the
Odes have posed serious problems for their interpreters.
There seems to be scholarly consensus on none of the major
questions. Bauer, Schulthess, Connolly, Frankenberg, and
Philonenko maintain that the Odes were originally composed in
Greek. Adam, Grant, Vööbus, Emerton, and Charlesworth insist
upon a Syriac original, while Carmignac opts for a Hebrew
original. Even those who agree upon a Syriac original cannot

1

agree upon whether the Odes were written in Antioch or in Edessa. Harris believes that the Odes came from a Jewish-Christian community. Harnack and Spitta see them as Jewish hymns which Christians have edited and altered. Labourt and Batiffol believe they come from a Gentile Christian background, and Frankenberg points to ties with Alexandrian theology. Conybeare and Fries characterize the Odes as Montanist, while Gunkel, Gressman, Kroll, Hora, Schlier, Dibelius, and Abramowski label them as "gnostic," though it is not clear that they all mean the same thing by the term. In more recent research Schenke, Grant, Rudolph and Jonas stress the similarities which they see between the Odes and various sorts of "gnostic" literature. While granting that the Odes are tributary to gnosticism, Charlesworth, Chadwick, Burkitt, Braun, Daniélou, and Worrell do not think it is accurate to characterize the Odes as fully gnostic.

Harnack, Bauer, and Bultmann all underline the importance of the Odes for understanding the Gospel of John, though Dodd, Barrett, and Brown scarcely mention them at all. Charlesworth suggests that the Odes and John reflect the same milieu, probably somewhere in Western Syria, and that ". . . both were probably composed in the same community. Continued research may eventually indicate that the Odist had been an Essene, who composed the Odes in the 'Johannine' community or school."[2] Tosato, Murray, Corwin, and Daniélou all take a similar position. Corwin suggests in her study of Ignatius of Antioch that Ignatius, John's Gospel, and the Odes all develop within the same cultural and spiritual milieu, and that all three show an undeniable resemblance to the imagery of the Thanksgiving Hymns from Qumran Cave I and the early pseudepigrapha.[3]

No agreement exists among scholars regarding the exact dating of the Odes, though most lean toward a date between the late first and end of the second century A.D. Drijvers maintains that the language of the Odes reflects second century Antiochene theology and shows the influence of Tatian's Diatessaron and Encratite ideas.[4] Since, he claims, one can also see in the Odes sophisticated attacks both on Mani and his community and on Marcionite teachings, a date of about

A.D. 275 seems likely, and Edessa, a city with both an important Manichaean community and a large number of Marcionites,
would be the most probable candidate for the place of their
composition.[5] McNeil contends, however, that it is not
possible to systematize the theology or the Christology of the
Odes in either an orthodox or heretical sense.[6] Brock accu-
rately summarizes the present state of our understanding of
the Odes: "The Odes of Solomon are one of the most beautiful
and, at the same time, most puzzling products of early Christianity. Provenance, date, and original language all remain
uncertain, despite 60-odd years of scholarly discussion on the
subject."[7]

Current scholarship on the Odes has limited itself
largely to the task of providing a critical text and new
translations. In 1973 Charlesworth published an eclectic text
given in vocalized Serto script together with a translation, a
brief introduction, and short interpretive notes.[8] M. Lattke
published a useful edition of the Odes in 1979. The first
volume contains a introductory study of the manuscripts and
makes available the full Coptic, Greek, and Syriac texts with
parallel German translations. The second volume consists of a
complete concordance of the Greek, Syriac, Coptic, and Latin
vocabulary occurring in the Odes. In 1980 Lattke published a
supplementary volume containing the Syriac text of the Odes in
Estrangela script and a facsimile of the Greek text of Ode
11.[9] Facsimiles of Papyrus Bodmer XI, Codex Askewianus, Codex
Nitriensis, and Cod. Syr. 9 in the John Rylands Library have
also been published by J. H. Charlesworth.[10] The most recent
translations are those of Per Beskow and Sten Hidal,[11] and of
J. Guirau and A. G. Hamman.[12]

In the existing research the primary method employed has
been the collection and analysis of terms, imagery and vocabulary and a search for parallels in the religious and philoso-
phical literature of the period. The value of this approach
for an exegesis of the Odes can be very great indeed. The
findings of such research can sometimes enable us to explain
obscure vocabulary and allusions. Yet all too often sweeping
and ill-founded conclusions have been made, based on parallels

of language and form that are either so strained or so common
as to be of little real significance. In their efforts to
establish the setting, external causes, influences, and
general cultural and religious climate, scholars of the Odes
have not infrequently neglected a careful study of the language, form and content of the texts of the Odes themselves.

A second approach, one which has been used rarely, is to
try to ascertain the practices or doctrines against which the
Odes are reacting. Drijvers maintains, "Fast alle überliefer-
ten Schriften des Urchristentums aus dem zweiten und dritten
Jahrhundert haben einen apologetischen und polemischen Charakter, und die Oden sind von dieser Regel keine Ausnahme."[13]

Thirdly, a few studies devoted to the hymnic passages in
the New Testament use the Odes as parallels to aid in interpretation. If these studies employ formcriticism, then
occasional observations of a formcritical nature may be made
concerning the Odes. Obviously such studies do not concen-
trate on the Odes but are interested only in those Odes which
appear to shed some light directly on the problems of interpretation of New Testament passages.

As far as I have been able to ascertain, no serious attempt has been made to apply systematically the methods of
formcriticism to the Odes. In his classic study of early
Christian hymnody, published over sixty years ago, J. Kroll
tried to classify the Odes according to the Gattungen of the
Old Testament Psalter.[14] He classifies most of the Odes as
Hymns of Praise, but understands Odes 21, 25, and 29 as Songs
of Thanksgiving, and Ode 5 as a Lament. Building upon the
philological work of E. Norden, he observes that the Odes, as
a collection, evidence characteristics of what he calls the
"Prose-hymn": long, asyndetically placed participial or relative predications, "you-style" or "he-style," nominal predica-
tion expanded by the use of relative clauses, parallelismus
membrorum, antithesis and the use of picturesque language.

Kroll analyzes only a few of the Odes and does little
more than point to similarities and differences vis-à-vis the
Old Testament Gattungen. He is not able to account for the
content and forms which do not fit the classical patterns. He

cannot, for example, explain the presence of material which
appears to be of a didactic nature, nor is he able to posit a
convincing purpose (or purposes) which would provide suitable
settings for the Odes. He maintains that the images and ideas
characteristic of the Odes belong to the "gnostic movement"
though they do not reflect a fixed or systematized stage in
its history. In any case, he believes, they could have had no
place in the "gemeinchristliche Kirche." Contemporary scholars would, of course, have difficulties with Kroll's distinc-
tions and definitions, more aware as they are than were their
predecessors, of the problems of evaluating and labeling
developments in early Christianity.

A few years later, in 1936, Abramowski maintained that
since he discerned no apparent order in the collection of the
Odes, it was necessary to use Gunkel's Gattungen research as
an organizing principle for a study of the Odes.[15] He classifies Odes 32, 34, 33, 16, 12, 23, 24, 31, 20, 19.6ff as
"Lehrdichtungen"; Odes 1, 3, 7, 10, 11, 12.1-3, 15, 16.1-7,
17, 18.1-10, 19.1-5, 20, 27, 35, 36, 38, 42 as "Individualoden in Psalmstil"; Ode 14 as "reines Bittgebet"; and Ode 25
as "reines Dankgebet." Abramowski's classifications are not
Gattungen in Gunkel's sense. They fail to offer us much help
in understanding the Odes and their origins because they lack
the necessary rigor and precision that belong to careful
formcritical analysis.

In 1965 G. Schille, in his monograph, Frühchristliche
Hymnen, proposed to classify according to Gattungen various
New Testament and early Christian texts which he regarded as
hymns.[16] Hymns belonging to a specific Gattung must share
common forms and motifs. One should be able to propose a
particular liturgical situation which inspired a particular
Gattung. He proposes the Gattung "Redeemer-Song," a subset of
which is the "Cross-Triumph-Song," see, for example, Odes 22,
31.1-5, 39.9-12, 41.11-12. He considers Odes 41.3-6, 21, 25,
35, 36, 37, 10, 31.8ff "Baptismal Songs"; Odes 15, 11, 27, 28,
29, 35-38, 17, 42 "Initiation Hymns," both groups belonging to
the broader Gattung "Initiation Song." Odes 9, 8, 20, 12,
30-34 are, according to Schille, "Revelation Songs."

Schille does not set out to study the Odes as such in any
great detail. He states in the introduction to his book that
he regards his work as a "Vorarbeit für eine umfassende Hymnodik des Neuen Testamentes."[17] Accordingly, no Ode is given
the extended treatment a formcritical study of the collection
would require. Schille's proposed Gattungen deserve serious
consideration, though we will not always be able to agree with
his allocation of individual Odes to particular Gattungen, nor
with the liturgical Sitz im Leben he posits for the Gattungen.
Indeed, even the Gattungen themselves rarely meet the exacting
criteria which Schille adopts from Gunkel.

Our understanding of the New Testament hymnic fragments,
the Hôdāyôt and Psalms of Solomon has been advanced substan-
tially thanks to recent formcritical investigations. Yet 72
years after their discovery by Harris and 48 years after the
publication of Gunkel's Einleitung in die Psalmen, we still
lack a study of the Odes carried out according to the methods
of formcriticism. As Abramowski noted, the agenda Gunkel set
for himself as he began his study of the canonical Psalms, is
the agenda still facing us when we take up the study of the
Odes.

What is needed, then, is the examination of the collection and a grouping together of those Odes which share a
common stock of ideas, motifs, images, and which exhibit a
basic similarity of structure, vocabulary and syntax. Establishing Gattungen according to the discipline of formcriticism
would provide us with tools for understanding the structure,
purpose and history of individual Odes and the forms contained
within them. Moreover, a successful isolating of individual
Gattungen and an analysis of the Odes according to formcritical methodology should eventually provide us with some information concerning the sort of community and setting from which
the Odes come, and some clearer indication of the place of the
Odes in the history of religious thought during the early
centuries of Christianity.

A careful formcritical analysis of the Odes demands what
the New Critics would call a "close reading of the text," that
is, a concern for the choice of vocabulary, syntax, point of

view, ". . . patterns of imagery, use of metaphors, and the type of interplay between words that generates wit, paradox and irony."[18] This task is hampered by the fact that the Syriac of the Odes is almost certainly from no earlier than the fourth century. Because of the peculiarities of the history of Syriac language, we cannot reconstruct the original structure and form of language which stood behind our Syriac version.[19] It remains true, nonetheless, that scholars of the Odes have not been sufficiently sensitive to the formal rhetorical devices used in the Odes as we have them, for example: repetitions, change of speaker, various sorts of parallelism, use of particles, and the configuration of component parts to indicate turning points and climaxes.

Research in the Odes should, of course, make serious efforts to identify what pre-existing units of tradition, if any, have found their way into an individual Ode. The individual Ode, however, must also be regarded and studied in its own precise and unique formulation. Gunkel stresses that although there is much in the canonical Psalms that is obviously dictated by the traditional Gattungen, although there is much that is impersonal, inherited, one nevertheless finds enormous variety and genuinely personal material that cannot be explained away merely by positing certain cultic or communal Sitz im Leben.[20] The individual Old Testament psalmist had a measure of freedom of expression, his own opportunity for artistry. The same is true for the author or authors of the Odes.

It would be foolish to deny that Frederick William Faber, George Herbert, or Charles Wesley depended upon the traditional language of Christian piety, especially the Scripture, or to refuse to recognize how the occasions for which they composed shaped their hymns. Yet it would be just as shortsighted to deny to each of these hymn-writers his own personal genius, his own poetic achievement. The Odes of Solomon, both in regard to form and to content, have their own characteristic stamp. They cannot be dismissed as products of a late stage in the development of the psalm-form, when the traditional Gattungen were blending into one another, when the

identifiable forms of the Old Testament Psalms were dissolving
and combining. The questions of formcriticism and literary
criticism need to be addressed to the Odes so that we can come
to a clearer understanding of the purpose and message of the
Odes and of the practice and faith of the community and
author(s) which are reflected in this collection.

In the following chapters I present studies of four of
the Odes of this collection. I attempt to demonstrate the
type of analysis which is appropriate to the Odes and which
must ultimately be applied to all the Odes if we are ever to
be able to understand them individually, to group them into
intelligible Gattungen, and to answer the difficult questions
of Introduction. In the concluding chapter I propose direc-
tions for further study, suggesting possible groupings for
some of the Odes, and illustrating in the case of one of these
groups how the isolation of a Gattung can aid us in the
interpretation of the Odes belonging to that Gattung.

CHAPTER II

Ode 36

1.   The Spirit of the Lord rested on me,
     and it lifted me up to the high place,

2.   And set me on my feet in the high place of the Lord,
     Before His fullness and His glory,
     While I was praising (Him) by the composition of
                                         His Odes.

3.   (The Spirit) brought me forth before the face of the
                                         Lord,
     And though I was a man,
     I was named a brilliant son of God,

4.   While I was praising among the praising ones,
     And I (was) a great one among the great ones.

5.   For according to the greatness of the Most High so it
                                         (the Spirit) made me,
     And according to His renewing He renewed me.

6.   And He anointed me with His perfection
     And I became one of those who are near Him.

7.   And my mouth was opened like a cloud of dew,
     And my heart gushed forth, a gusher of righteousness.

8.   And my approach was in peace,
     and I was established by the Spirit of providence.

Hallelujah!

In Ode 36 the speaker, referring to himself in the third
person masculine singular, reports an experience which has
occurred in the past. In vss 1-2b he is the object of actions
taken by the "Spirit of the Lord." The verbs are all in the
perfect tense. The speaker is the subject in vs 2c, where his
activity, introduced by the conjunction kd, is described as
present or contemporaneous with the preceding action.

The subject of the feminine singular third person perfect
verb in vs 3a is not specified, but it is reasonable to assume
that the Spirit is once again the subject. The dependent
clause in vs 3b, introduced by wkd, has the speaker as its
subject, and he is the subject as well of the first person
singular ethpeᶜel perfect in 3c, the ethpeᶜel having the force
of the passive in Syriac. Vs 4 is introduced by kd, and like
vs 3, whose first three words it repeats verbatim, uses the
participle plus the personal pronoun, with the speaker as the
antecedent.

The perfect verb in vs 5a requires a third person feminine singular subject, while the parallel perfect verb in vs
5b requires a third person singular masculine subject. From
the context we may understand the Spirit as subject in 5a and
the Most High in 5b. The subject of the third person masculine singular perfect verb in vs 6a is not specified, but is
probably the Most High. Vs 6b describes what the speaker "has
become"; he is the only logical subject of the first person
singular perfect verb.

The events of vss 7-8 are also described as having taken
place in the past, the perfect tense being employed. In vss
7-8a the subjects are modified by a first person singular
possessive pronominal suffix, referring back to the speaker,
who is also the subject of the ethpeᶜel perfect in vs 8b,
while the Spirit of providence is the agent of the action.

Ode 36 consists of the speaker's report in the first
person singular of the events surrounding his ascent to
heaven, to the presence of the Lord. His report is prefaced
by no introductory thanksgiving formula, it concludes with no
expression of thanks or praise. It contains neither petition
nor any formula of praise directly addressed to the Lord; it

contains no exhortations, call to praise, invitation explicitly directed to an audience. On the basis of the text of Ode
36 neither the intention of the speaker in formulating the
poem nor the use it might once have served in the community
which collected the Odes is clear. Like so many Odes in this
collection, Ode 36 consists almost entirely of an individual
speaker's account of what the Lord has done for him.

The speaker expresses himself in the style of Semitic
poetry familiar to us from the Old Testament Psalms, the
Psalms of Solomon and the Hôdāyôt of Qumran. The author uses
no elaborate mythological language, he avoids the sort of
elaborate descriptions of the heavenly world we find in
apocalyptic literature. There are no descriptions of what he
sees along the way, no hostile powers hindering his advance,
no angelic helpers or interpreters, no heavenly mysteries or
cosmological secrets revealed, no lasting consequences for
others, for example, the opening of locked doors or of gates
to secure access for those who are to follow. The ascent by
the Spirit is simply the means whereby the Odist arrives at
the heights, to the Lord's presence. What transpires in the
presence of the Most High receives the bulk of the author's
attention.

Verse 1

The verb in vs 1a, ʾttnyht, is the ethpeʿel perfect of
the root nwh, and with the preposition ʿl it means "to settle
upon," "to rest on," "to press heavily upon" (Payne Smith
[Comp], 331). It is difficult to understand in what sense the
speaker could describe himself as having "settled upon" the
Spirit of the Lord.[1] The verb can be construed as either the
first person singular perfect or the third person feminine
singular perfect. If we take it as the latter, the Spirit of
the Lord could be understood as the subject, and if we emend
ʿl to ʿly, as J. Strugnell suggests,[2] the line would read,
"The Spirit of the Lord rested upon me," reminiscent of Is
11.2.

Verse 2

The goal of the speaker's ascent is to come into the
presence of the Lord, for "in the high place of the Lord" he
was placed, "Before His fullness and His glory." Some scholars interpret šwmly' as equivalent to the heavenly world, the
plērōma,[3] but the qualification of "fullness as "His," and the
parallel expression, "His glory," argue that we should understand both terms as qualities of God which represent the
divine presence.[4]

The precise sense of vs 2c is difficult to ascertain,
because of the obscurity inherent in the conjunction kd. The
line either means that once the speaker was brought up to the
divine presence, he was praising (the Lord) by the composition
of His odes,[5] or that while he was so doing, the Spirit of the
Lord rested upon him and caused him to ascend to the presence
of the Lord in heaven.[6] In either case, the speaker identifies himself as one who composes, not merely recites odes.

Verse 3

Charlesworth follows Mingana and Harris in inserting the
editorial note, "Christ Speaks," between vss 1-2 and vss 3-8,
though Christ is nowhere mentioned in the Ode.[7] The Spirit is
probably the subject in vs 3a, as suggested; she is responsible for bringing forth the speaker, yldtny; she is the agent
of his renewal before the face of the Lord.[8] According to vss
3b-c the speaker received a new status, he was given a new
name, "the son of God," brh d'lh'. There is no reason immediately to equate this name with the Christological title in the
New Testament as applied to Jesus of Nazareth. The term has a
rich history and an extensive background in the Old Testament
and in Jewish apocryphal literature, as well as in the divi
filius or theou hyious language of the Hellenistic world.[9]
The titles brh dy 'l and br 'lywn also appear in a Palestinian
Aramaic text found at Qumran, 4QpsDanA, where they are used in
a setting that is clearly apocalyptic, and probably used of
some expected figure.[10] In Joseph and Asenath Joseph is
called ho hyios tou theou ho prōtotokos (21.3) not only
because of his supernatural beauty and wisdom, but also, as M.

Hengel claims, "This is probably meant to express the thought
that he belongs to the sphere of God; one might even talk of
his 'angelic character'."[11] Hengel also points out that in
later Talmudic texts the charismatic wonder-worker or the
mystic who was raised to the divine presence was often designated "son" by God, even addressed as "my son."[12] The title,
"son of God," Hengel maintains, ". . . must have played some
role in the charismatic and mystical circles of Palestinian
Judaism."[13] In Ode 36.1-3 the speaker has been raised to
God's presence, has experienced renewal, has been named "the
son of God." It will become evident in examining the remaining vss of the Ode that the speaker regards himself as having
been made one of the heavenly or angelic beings. In the
present context, being named "son of God" can probably be
interpreted as referring to the transformation of the speaker
into a heavenly or angelic being. The new status of the
speaker is stressed by the formulation of vs 3b: "Though I
was a man," kd here being understood in an adversative
sense.[14]

     There is sharp division of opinion among scholars on how
to render the word nhyr² in vs 3c,[15] and just as much dis-
agreement on its connotations and religious background.[16]
Curiously, none of the commentators connects this term with
the expectation prominent in apocryphal writers, that the
blessed would be transformed into angelic beings who are
described as "brilliant," "shining," "luminous."[17] It is
possible that this term, along with "the son of God," is used
to describe the transformation the speaker undergoes in the
presence of the Most High.

Verse 4

     This verse, introduced once again by kd, describes the
speaker as "praising," mšbh among those who are praising,
mšbh².[18] The point of the verse is that now the speaker is
numbered among "those who praise," or as the parallel line, vs
4b, puts it, that he is one of the rwrbh², "the great," "the
princes," "the chiefs." Both expressions probably refer to
angelic figures.[19]

Verse 5

The subject of vs 5a is not supplied in the text, but
"the Spirit" is a likely subject for the feminine singular
perfect verb ʿbdtny, "she made me," for it was the Spirit,
presumably, who bore the speaker in vs 3a, yldtny. It is not
at all clear in what sense the speaker was made "according to
the greatness of the Most High," though note the use of the
root rb, both here, "greatness," rbwth, and in "great, rb
among the great ones, rwrbnʾ," in the preceding line, vs 4b.[20]
The verb form in vs 5b, as it presently stands, presumes a
change in speaker; hdtny requires a masculine singular
subject. Since the Most High is mentioned in vs 5a, it is
probably He who is intended as the subject of vs 5b. The
precise sense of "according to His renewing" is also
obscure.[21]

Verse 6

The Most High is probably also the subject who anoints
the speaker with His fullness or perfection, mšmlywth, with
the result that the speaker becomes one of those who are near
Him, qrybwhy.[22] In apocryphal literature, the seer is frequently anointed upon his arrival in heaven and preceding his
transformation into an angelic being.[23]

Verse 7

This verse seems to describe what occurred after the
speaker entered the divine presence and became an angelic
being. The speaker describes himself as "praising" with the
angelic beings in vs 4, and perhaps praising is what he
describes himself as doing in vs 7.[24] The similes in this
verse are, however, obscure and difficult to interpret.[25]
Perhaps what is being underlined in vs 7a is the divine origin
or cause of the events mentioned in the line: as God causes
the cloud to open and rain down dew, so He causes the mouth of
the speaker to open and to pour forth praise or perhaps
prophecy.

Verse 8

The Ode concludes with the speaker describing his

"access," his "being brought near," qwrb᾽, a term which may
summarize the entire process of ascent and coming before the
Lord. The approach is characterized as one which took place
bšlm᾽, "in peace," "in well-being."[26] The speaker may mean
that he was brought to the Lord's presence without danger,
that his arrival took place safely, without any difficulties,
or the term may be construed as carrying the connotations of
the blessings of eschatological salvation.[27]

According to the loose parallelism of the verse, his
being brought near is comparable to his being "established,
settled, firmly set," ᾽štrrt.[28] As it was the Spirit of the
Lord who rested upon him, and who lifted him up and placed him
in the divine presence, as it was the Spirit, presumably, who
bore him and made him (vss 3,5), so it is the Spirit who is
identified as the agent by whom he was established, brought
near in peace. The Spirit is here characterized as the Spirit
of providence, mdbrnwt᾽; it is the Spirit who has brought
about the events described, the Spirit who acts according to
the plan or providence of the Lord.

The motif of ascent to the heavens has a long and complex
history and was particularly popular in late antiquity. In
that period of religious syncretism the motif of ascent to the
heavens could be used to serve widely different purposes and
have different meanings, depending upon the specific context
in which it was employed. It is necessary to survey the
various schemata in which the motif is used to discover the
proper context in which to interpret Ode 36.

1.   Soul's ascent into the heavens after death.

In the Hellenistic world, it was often believed that
after death the individual's soul would arise and ascend to
the heavens.[29] This belief took on a special significance
among Christians who desired to ascend to the heavens either
immediately after death in imitation of, or following after
Jesus who showed them the way.[30] Within schools of gnostic
thought the ascent of the soul after death was the main
prospect held out to the gnostic, for it represented the
reversal of the astral descent or fall of the soul into the

cosmos.[31]   Though all the events described in Ode 36 could be
regarded as taking place after the soul is freed from the body
and ascends to the heavens after death, it is noteworthy that
the speaker never in fact alludes to death.   Unlike the
gnostic myth, there is no indication whatsoever that the soul
is returning to its home, that it is ascending to the place
from which it once descended, that it is regaining its true
acosmic nature.

2.   Ascent of the gnostic redeemer figure.[32]

     According to the basic lines of this mythic schema, whose
origins and precise relationship to Christianity are still
uncertain,[33] the redeemer figure is a pre-existent heavenly
being who descends into the cosmos to awaken "pneumatics" to
the truth of their heavenly origin and to save these pre-
existent souls by collecting them and leading them upwards,
thus to reconstitute the Primal Man or to reintegrate the
divine totality.   The redeemer figure himself ascends into the
heavens, returning to his heavenly point of departure.[34]   Ode
36, if it is dependent upon this myth as it has been recon-
structed, offers a version that is so truncated that its
relationship to the myth is no longer recognizable with any
certainty.   There is no mention in Ode 36 of the redeemer
figure's descent from the heavenly world, nor is there any
reference to any work of his before the ascent.[35]   The
redeemer-ascent schema, moreover, does not adequately account
for the events Ode 36 describes as transpiring in the presence
of the Most High as the climax of the ascent account.

3.   Ascent of divine Wisdom.[36]

     The Jewish myth of the descent and reascent of personi-
fied Wisdom is found in various forms in a number of sapien-
tial texts.[37]   Though we would not expect the righteous man
(or his soul) to share in all the qualities or works of
Wisdom, there is no indication that the speaker in Ode 36,
however, represents in any way a personification or embodiment
of divine Wisdom.   He has none of its characteristics.   He
makes no claim to have enjoyed an intimate pre-existent union

with God as, e.g., His breath, image, or companion. He is not
identified with the divine Spirit, indeed, the Spirit of the
Lord is obviously a distinct figure in the Ode. The speaker
is neither instrumental in the creation of the world nor does
he communicate wisdom or revelation to men. All we have in
Ode 36 is the ascent and the events which take place before
the divine presence, and it is precisely ascent which is
generally absent from Wisdom texts.[38] The main point of Ode
36 is the transformation which the speaker undergoes, while
Wisdom remains from start to finish her transcendent heavenly
self.

4.   Ascent as return to heaven of a divine visitor.[39]

That divine figures could descend and mingle among men,
and subsequently ascend back to their heavenly homes was
widely accepted in late antiquity. Stories abound of gods
visiting in human disguise,[40] and there is abundant evidence
of men claiming to be such divine figures; see, for example,
Lucian of Samosata's accounts of Alexander of Abonuteichos and
of Peregrinus.[41] That supernatural figures could come to
earth disguised as men was an accepted part of Jewish legend
as well. The tradition is found quite explicitly in Abraham's
reception of heavenly guests in Gen 18 and in the story of
Tobias, but throughout the Old Testament there are stories of
God acting through angels or messengers.[42]

The speaker in Ode 36, however, does not depict himself
as a heavenly visitor, an angel in human disguise; on the
contrary, in vs 3b he insists that at the time of his ascent
and renewal he was simply a man, brnš'. There is no indication that the ascent represents his return to his heavenly
home, nor is there any report of his activities on earth
preceding the ascent.

5.   Ascent as apotheosis.

Apotheosis is the ascent, following the death of an
illustrious person, which represents his being snatched away
from earth and his admission to the heavenly court.[43] Having
lived an exceptional life such a person is rewarded with

immortality and divinity. In Ode 36 there is, as noted
earlier, no indication that the action described in the Ode
takes place after or in place of the speaker's death, nor is
there any suggestion that he has performed heroic or exceptional deeds which have led up to the reward of immortality.
Indeed, the events described in Ode 36.3-8 are not depicted as
"rewards", nor is there any report of the deified man's
subsequent deeds for men's benefit.

6.   The individual gnostic's spiritualized ascent.
     Hans Jonas explains,

> In a later stage of "gnostic" development . . . the
> external topology of the ascent through the spheres,
> with the successive divesting of the soul of its
> worldly envelopments and the regaining of its
> original acosmic nature, could be "internalized" and
> find its analogue in a psychological technique of
> inner transformations by which the self, while still
> in the body, might attain the Absolute as an imma-
> nent, if temporary condition: an ascending scale of
> mental states replaces the stations of the mythical
> itinerary: the dynamics of progressive spiritual
> self-transformation, the spatial thrust through the
> heavenly spheres.[44]

The purpose of ascent in Ode 36 is not a gnostic deliverance
of the speaker from the bonds of earthly existence. The
material universe is not presented as worthless, demonic,
opposed to the divine. There is no hint of the speaker
passing through an ascending scale of mental states, and the
Ode's ascent has nothing to do with a process of "increasing
self-unification and mental abstraction," such as is found in
Nag Hammadi tractates Allogenes, Zostrianos, or The Three
Steles of Seth.[45] In Ode 35, though the speaker depends upon
the agency of the Most High and the Spirit of the Lord, though
he undergoes transformation, there is no redeemer figure who
represents the upper part of a divided soul, whose lower part,
in such a scheme, would be the Odist. The ascent and transformation, then, does not represent the restoration of the
speaker's true self previously imprisoned in matter, nor a
reunification with his divine self.[46] There is nothing
gnostic about the speaker's ascent in Ode 36.

Wilhelm Bousset notes that the myth of the divine redeemer's journey from heaven into the depths of the world or
even into the depths of Hades and back again to heaven became
a symbol that served as an example or illustration for the
salvation of the individual believer.[47]   He remarks:

> The believer is united with the saving deity and
> experiences with the deity all the terror of the
> journey to Hades and all the triumph in the victory
> over the demons; with the redeemer god the believer
> also experiences the heavenward journey, the appear-
> ance before God's throne, the triumphing and rejoin-
> ing in heaven.[48]

He regards Ode 36 as a particularly good example of just such
an application of the redeemer myth to the fate of the individual redeemed soul. He observes that here, as elsewhere in the
Odes, the "I" of the speaker is "completely merged with the
Messiah, so that in a particular case one hardly knows who is
spoken of."[49]   Helmut Koester agrees ". . . that in those Odes
formulated in the I-style, the person of the revealer often
flows together with the person of the believer."[50]   As for Ode
36, Koester's judgement echoes that of Bousset: "Through rebirth, the redeemed becomes identical with the redeemer.
. . ."[51]

The speaker in Ode 36 surely undergoes a transformation,
but it is not self-evident that the speaker is changed into or
merges with "Christ" or some redeemer figure, or that he is
sharing in the fate of a descending-ascending redeemer.

7. Ascent of the Jewish apocalyptic visionary or Merkavah
    mystic.[52]
    When compared with the apocalyptic literature of the
period extending from the second century B.C. to the second
century A.D., Ode 36 stands out as quite distinctive. First,
the Odist describes his experiences simply in the first person
singular without identifying himself, and without assuming a
pseudonymous identity.[53]   The speaker makes no mention of any
specific reason for his ascent; he has none of the motives
which Susan Niditch has pointed out as common in the literature of the period.[54]   The ascent is preceded by no report of

personal crisis or sickness, there is no mention of any
community difficulties.[55] There is no indication that the
motivation for the ascent is the desire for some privileged
insight into God's secret plans for the Odist or his
community. In marked contrast to the visions, auditions,
heavenly journeys of the figures of apocalyptic literature,
the object of the ascent is not to gain access to the secrets
of the universe, to superhuman knowledge.[56]

    Niditch recognizes a basic ritual schema of preparation
for the vision or ascent consisting of the following elements:
1) retreat to an isolated location, 2) ascetical practices, 3)
employment of repeated actions, either gestures or prayers, 4)
awaiting a significant event, 5) loss of consciousness, e.g.,
"a kind of death and resurrection," 6) "an experience of
height or ascent."[57] Most of these elements also precede the
ascent of the mystic in the Hekhalot literature.[58] The
speaker in Ode 36 gives us no detailed description of his
preparations for the ascent, indeed, the emphasis is placed
upon the action of the Spirit in readying the speaker, in
bringing about the ascent. The speaker's composition of the
Lord's Odes could perhaps be construed as a preparatory
process which facilitates or induces the ascent to the
heavens.[59] It is equally possible, however, that the composing of Odes refers to inspired singing, whether in the context
of individual prayer or community worship, as the context of
the Odist's ascent, though not necessarily its precise cause.
As we shall see, ascent is frequently depicted as occurring
within the context of prayer or worship.

    Both the actual ascent and the climax of the ascent in
Ode 36 are quite unlike what we normally find in apocalyptic
and Merkavah texts. No attention is given to the actual
ascent; it is not presented as a journey through the
heavens.[60] Either the speaker does not see, or does not think
it important to mention seeing details of heavenly geography,
the places of reward and punishment, the heavenly palace of
God with its numerous chambers, or the chamber where the
winds, stars, and lightening are stored.[61]

Gruenwald notes that in the Jewish mystical tradition, as he traces it through both the apocalyptic and the Hekhalot literature, the visionary's experience basically followed the model of the vision of God in a human form that is found in the Old Testament, though each writer could add or subtract one or another element and embroider the account with various imaginative features.[62] The scriptural tradition 1) gave fire an important role in the vision, 2) depicted God as sitting on a throne, 3) appearing as a man, 4) residing in a palace, 5) accompanied by angels, 6) who sang hymns in His presence.[63] The only elements which are even alluded to in Ode 36 are numbers 5 and 6. It is significant, however, that the angelic or heavenly figures in Ode 36 are mentioned only in the context of the speaker's transformation or new identity: he was praising among the praising, great among the great (vs 4) and he became one of those who are near the Lord (vs 6). The point or goal of the speaker's ascent is not that he praises God with the angels, and certainly not that he receives knowledge, sees God or carries out some mediatorial services, for these are not even mentioned, but rather that, by the action of God and the Spirit, he has been transformed, he has been raised up to God's presence to enjoy a heavenly existence.

The notion of a seer joining the company of the heavenly beings, indeed, even becoming one like them, can be found in a number of apocalyptic texts. According to Ascension of Isaiah, as Isaiah ascended from heaven to heaven, "the glory of his countenance was being transformed" (7.25). In 2 Enoch 22 when Enoch reaches the tenth heaven, he falls to his face while the troops of cherubim and seraphim sing. Michael, according to the Lord's instructions, anoints him with oil shining like the sun and sweet as dew. Enoch realizes that he has been transformed: "And I looked at myself, and I was as one of the glorious ones, and there was no difference."

8. Ascent as realization of eschatological salvation.[64]

The transformation into heavenly or angelic beings which certain apocalyptic seers claim to have experienced in the

context of their ascent to God's presence is similar to what
is often described as the future state of the blessed.
According to 2 Bar 51.10ff:

> It shall come to pass when that appointed day has
>   gone by that . . .
> In the heights of that world shall they dwell,
> And they shall be made like unto the angels,
> And be made equal to the stars.
> And they shall be changed into every form they
>   desire
> From beauty into loveliness,
> And from light into the splendour of glory.

Similar hope is held out in 1 Enoch 104.2ff:

> Be hopeful; for aforetime ye were put to shame
> through ill and affliction; but now ye shall shine
> as the lights of heaven, ye shall shine and ye shall
> be seen, and the portals of heaven shall be opened
> to you. Be hopeful and cast not away your hope; for
> ye shall have great joy as the angels of heaven
> . . . ye shall become companions of the hosts of
> heaven.

In 1 Enoch 108.12ff the blessed shine (c.f. also 1 Enoch
104.2ff [above], 2 Bar 51.5, 49.2; 2 Enoch 22.8ff [above]; Esr
7.97, 66.7, 19.1; Wis 3.7, Dan 12.3):

> And I will bring forth in shining light those who
> loved my holy name, and I will seat each on the
> throne of his honour. And they shall be resplendent
> for times without number; for righteousness is the
> judgement of God; for to the faithful He will give
> faithfulness in the habitation of upright paths.
> And they shall see those who were born in darkness
> led into darkness, while the righteous shall be
> resplendent.

It seems to be in such a conception of eschatological
salvation that Ode 36's notions of ascent and subsequent
transformation are rooted. The speaker in the Ode could be
understood, then, to be describing himself as one who has been
numbered among the blessed, who has attained final salvation,
who has reached God's presence and who has been made into a
heavenly or angelic being. A study of Odes 11, 21, 35, and
38, in which the speaker also narrates in the first person
singular the events surrounding his ascent to heaven or
paradise confirms Aune's contention:

The effects which are attendant on this trip to the
celestial Paradise include those blessings which
Jewish eschatology expected to accompany the restoration of primal conditions in the future. . . .[65]

He lists: 1) freedom from disease and pain, 2) clothing with
a heavenly garment of light or immortality, 3) possession of
immortal or eternal life, 4) possession of a crown, 5) coming
before the Lord with the saved, 6) worship and praise of God
in the company of the angels in Paradise.[66] What are looked
forward to as the ultimate blessings promised to the saved in
apocalyptic literature, the Odist claims in Ode 36 and in the
other Odes of ascent, to have already enjoyed. In other
words, the speaker in Ode 36 claims that he has experienced
eschatological salvation. Aune, however, goes beyond the
evidence, at least the evidence we find in Ode 36, when he
claims that in the Odes, "Participation in this eschatological
salvation had been made possible by the Incarnation and
Ascension of the Messiah."[67] Ode 36 does not connect the
experience of the realization of eschatological salvation with
the Christian kerygma.

The literature of the Qumran community exhibits a realized eschatology similar to what we find in Ode 36.[68] In both
1QH 3.19-20 and 11.7-14 the author describes in the first
person singular how he has been transferred into the community
of the saved, united with the angels in their praise of God.[69]
According to 1QH 3.19-20 the Lord made him rise to the everlasting heights, and in 1QH 11.12 he is "raised from the dust
to the Lord's secrets of truth." As in Ode 36 there is in 1QH
no vision of God or any celestial sights. In 1QH 11.12 the
speaker recalls that he has entered into the communion with
the congregation of the Sons of heaven:

> And thou hast cast an everlasting destiny for man in
> company of the Spirits of knowledge, that he might
> praise thy name in joy[ful] concord and recount thy
> marvels before all thy works.

In 1QH 11.7-14 the speaker probably also alludes to entrance
into the community. The Lord cleansed him, made him holy,

> that this vermin that is man may be raised from the
> dust to [thy] secret [of truth] and from the spirit

of perversity to [thine] understanding and that he
may watch before thee with the everlasting host and
together with [thy] spirits of holiness that he may
be renewed with all [that is] [and] shall be and
with them that know, in common rejoicing.

M. Delcor argues that in 1QH 11.10.14 it is entrance into the
Qumran community that is described in terms of spiritual
resurrection, deliverance from a perverse spirit, being
present before God, being in communion with angels, and being
made a new creation.[70]

If we are correct in seeing Ode 36 as the speaker's
narration of his experience of eschatological salvation
realized in the present, then we must ask, 1) what is the
context in which the experience occurs, 2) what is the purpose
for which the Ode was intended?

1) Aune maintains, as we have noted, that the Odes are
set in the context of the cultic worship of the early Syriac
Christian community.[71] In its communal worship the community,
under the leadership of a cultic prophet, experiences a
corporate ascent into heaven.[72] The community experiences
itself as "present in the heavenly world in final worship of
God in the presence of angelic beings." As we have pointed
out, however, the point of Ode 36 is not so much the praise of
God, whether conceived of as occurring in heaven, on earth, or
in both places at once, but the transformation the Odist
undergoes as he is brought forth by the Spirit, the new status
he enjoys when he is brought before the Most High. What the
Odist becomes rather than what he does is the focus of Ode 36.
Moreover, it is far from clear in this Ode that the transformation which is described is a communal one. Verse 2c, if we
interpret it to mean that the Spirit raises the speaker while
he is praising God by composing His Odes, could be taken to
indicate that the ascent takes place within the context of the
speaker's composing of Odes in the community's worship, but it
might also refer to his private composition of Odes of praise
as an exercise of personal piety.[73]

In certain gnostic groups, in various mystery cults, in
Qumran, and perhaps in other Jewish groups,[74] the ascent into

heaven and the transformation into a heavenly or divine being
is frequently understood to be effected through ritual action.
Rebirth, renewal by the Spirit, reception of eternal life,
becoming immortal are all used in conjunction with initiation
in a wide range of religious groups in late antiquity.[75] Ode
36's use of terms like renewal, rebirth, anointing, being made
into a heavenly being might suggest that the ascent and transformation took place within the context of a liturgy of initiation.   Unfortunately, however, the Ode lacks references to
specific liturgical practices. If the speaker's experience of
ascent is connected with the liturgy of initiation or with any
other ritual, Ode 36 provides us with no univocal proof of the
fact, and with no hints as to the nature and scope of the
liturgical action.[76]

  2) As for the intent or purpose of the Ode, two general
possibilities exist. Either the Ode was written simply as
"private" poetry of devotion,[77] or it was designed to be used
in the liturgical life of the author's community. Perhaps we
can imagine a liturgical service (Christian or not) that
functions along the lines of the worship service to which Paul
alludes in 1 Cor 14. When the Corinthian community comes
together, "each one has a hymn, a lesson, a revelation, a
tongue or an interpretation." Perhaps Ode 36, though it does
not have any introductory thanksgiving formula, might be an
example of a charismatic thanksgiving song which could be
spoken by any member of the community who felt so inspired.
It is also possible that the author intended his poem to serve
not only to edify his own community, but also to make known
what sort of experience are available in his community and to
attract those outsiders who might be interested in finding a
way to the presence of God and to transformation into a
celestial being.

CHAPTER III

Ode 16

1. As the work of the ploughman is the plough,
   And the work of the pilot is the steering of the ship,
   So also my work is the singing of the Lord in His
   praises.

2. My craft and my labour are in His praises,
   Because His love provided for my heart,
   And up to my lips it poured forth fruits.

3. For my love is the Lord,
   Therefore I will sing to Him.

4. Indeed, I am strengthened by His praises,
   And I have faith in him.

5. I will open my mouth,
   And His Spirit will speak in me:
   The glory of the Lord and His beauty,

6. The work of His hands,
   And the labour of His fingers,

7. The abundance of His mercy,
   And the power of His word.

8. For the word of the Lord searches that which is not seen,
   And His thought that which is revealed.

9. For the eye sees His works,
   And the ear hears His thought.

10. He spread out the earth,
    And set the waters in the sea.

11. He stretched out the heaven,
    And set the stars in order.

12. And He set in order the creation and He established it,
     And He rested from His works.

13. And created things run in their courses,
     And work their works,
     And they do not know how to stop or to cease work,

14. And the hosts are subject to His word.

15. The treasury of light is the sun,
     And the treasury of darkness is the night.

16. The sun, then, makes the day become bright;
     The night, then, brings darkness over the face of the
                                                    earth.

17. And their acceptance (is) one from another;
     They tell of the beauty of God.

18. And there is not anything which (is) without the Lord,
     Because He had come to be
     Before anything came to be.

19. And the worlds come into being by His word,
     And by the thought of His heart.

20. Glory and honour to His name.

Hallelujah!

Ode 16 can be divided into two sections. In vss 1-7 the
speaker in the first person singular discusses his work of
singing of the Lord in His praises or hymns. In the first
verse the speaker compares his work to that of the ploughman
and of the ship's pilot. In vss 2-3 he discusses his motives
for singing of the Lord. In vs 4 he alludes to a particular
benefit he derives from the Lord's praises and in vs 5a-b he
claims the Spirit's inspiration for what he says or sings.
Vss 5c-7 enumerate the topics or the subject matter of his
inspired speech or singing, centering on the Lord's work and
labour in creation. Kittel regards vss 1-7 as a personal
confession by the Odist which could function as an independent
song in which the speaker addresses the subject: why I must
praise God and sing to Him.[1] He suggests that it could also
be an introduction to a thoroughly personal song about the
great and glorious things God has accomplished for the speaker. Whether or not vss 1-7 ever enjoyed an independent
existence or was at some point an introduction to another poem
cannot be established. The repetition of "His word," mlth, at
the conclusion of vs 7b and at the beginning of vs 8a may,
however, reveal a seam in the composition of the Ode, i.e.,
the repetition may represent a deliberate editorial attempt to
cement two originally independent pieces.[2]

As it now stands vss 1-7 function as an introduction to a
longer didactic poem extending from vs 8 to vs 20 in which the
"I" of the speaker disappears completely. Rather than being a
"personal confession," vss 1-7 probably should be seen as a
conventional claim of inspiration. Kittel and Abramowski
characterize vss 8-20 of Ode 16 as a "creation poem,"[3] while
Gunkel dubs it a "nature psalm."[4] While the Odist obviously
depends upon Old Testament models, especially Pss 8 and 19,
vss 8-20 have their own structure and theme. Sandwiched
between statements describing God's work in creation, vss
10-22a, 18-19, vss 13-17 describe how created things work (vs
13), how the heavenly hosts are subject to the word of the
Lord (vs 14), how the sun and the night tell the beauty of God
by doing the work assigned to them (vss 15-17). In the
present structure of the Ode perhaps vss 8-20 are meant to be

seen as an example of the sort of "hymn" or "praise" the
speaker voices, though the only explicit expression of praise
is the concluding doxology, and though it is without any
formula of introduction. The meaning and function of vss 8-9
are problematic and will be taken up in the commentary.

Whatever the history of the components of this Ode, the
author has forged the traditions available to him into a
unified composition having the dual theme of work and praise.
He has skillfully interwoven the two themes. According to vss
1-7 his work is to sing the Lord's praises, to speak His
praise or glory and His beauty (vs 5), to tell of the work
that the Lord has done in creation. The didactic poem not
only recalls the Lord's and His word's work, for which He is
worthy of praise, but also recalls that of creation, which, as
we noted, gives praise, tells His beauty (vs 17) precisely by
doing its work. The concluding doxology fittingly proclaims
praise or glory to the Lord's name.

Verse 1

The Ode begins with a simile in which the speaker compares his work with that of a ploughman and of a pilot.[5]
Repeating the root ʿbd, work, in each of the tricola, in vs 1c
he identifies his own work as singing, mzmwrʾ, of the Lord by
His praises or hymns, tšbḥth. The exact point of the simile
is unclear.[6] Perhaps he has been influenced by Sir 38 where
the speaker describes in the third person singular the activity of the scribe, the student of divine wisdom, comparing his
work to that of the ploughman, the craftsman, the smith, and
the potter. The ploughman and the pilot are a natural pair to
set in parallelism since they both serve as guides; they are
both responsible for setting and regulating direction and
movement.[7] Is it too fanciful to see in the simile a possible
allusion to the responsibility of guiding and directing a
group in its liturgical gatherings?[8] Or does the speaker wish
to identify himself as one who composes mzmwrʾ, like the wise
man in Sir 39.6; 15.10; 44.4-5? If he composes psalms for the
Lord, are they intended for public community worship or as an
exercise of private devotion, or might they be designed for

use in conjunction with some study situation?[9] No matter how
we interpret the introductory simile and the precise sense of
1c, it is important to note that here, and continuing through
vss 2-7, the speaker reflects upon his own activity or work as
one who sings or composes "praises."

Verse 2

In vs 2a the speaker repeats the thought of vs 1c, with
the emphasis that poetic hendiadys ("my craft and my labour")
effects: his work is His (presumably the Lord is antecedent
of the possessive adjective) praises or hymns, as in 1c,
tšbhth. Vss 2b-c, introduced by mtwl d, explains the reason
or points to the source of the speaker's praises. The speaker
employs two metaphors, and describes with perfect verbs how he
has come to voice the Lord's praises or hymns. According to
vs 2b the Lord's love, hwb', nourished or provided for his
heart. In vs 2c the speaker's heart is the subject, and it is
reported to have poured forth, gs', fruits. "Fruits" here
probably refers to the hymns or praises of the Lord which have
their source in the speaker's heart.[10]

Verse 3

Catchwords connect this verse with the two which precede
it; the speaker returns to the present tense and declares that
the Lord is his love, hwby (c.f. vs 2b), and in vs 3b promises
with the first person imperfect verb that he will therefore
sing to Him, ' zmr (c.f. vs 1c, mzmwr').[11] By repetition of
the love motif the speaker underlines that love is the motive
and the ground for His praises.[12]

Verse 4

The Odist continues discussing "His praises," tšbhth, in
vs 4a, but now states that he himself benefits from the Lord's
praises: he is strengthened by them. Vs 4b is probably meant
to be taken together with vs 4a to mean that the speaker's
hymnwt', his trust or confidence or faith in the Lord, is
stimulated, braced by the praises he offers to the Lord.

Verse 5

Returning to the imperfect, the speaker repeats in new
terms the message of 3b: he declares his intent to "open his
mouth," presumably in hymns or praises.[13] In vs 5b there is
an important shift in subject: it is now "His Spirit," who
will speak in the speaker. The speaker thus expresses his
conviction that when he opens his mouth in the Lord's praises,
it is really the Lord's Spirit who speaks in and through
him.[14] What the Lord's Spirit will say in the speaker is the
tšbwht² of the Lord, here meaning "praise," synonymous with
"glory," as an attribute of the Lord. Indeed, its use with
"His beauty," y²ywth, in vs 5b probably represents another
instance of the writer's special fondness for the use of
pleonasm.

Verse 6

Vs 6a parallels "glory of the Lord," and vs 6b parallels
"His beauty," and like them are objects of the verb "will
speak" in vs 5b. They probably refer to what the Lord accomplished in His work of creation. Tsakona (324) regards vs 6
as a combination of Ps 8.3a, "When I look at the heavens, the
work of your fingers," and Ps 102.25, "Of old thou didst lay
the foundations of the earth, and the heavens, the works of
your hands," and suggests therefore, that the Odist is referring to the creation of the heavens in this verse. However,
in Job 34.19 human beings, rich and poor, are called the
"works of his hands," and in Is 66.2 earth and the heavens are
referred to as "these things my hands have made," and in Ps
96.5 "his hands" formed the dry land.[15]

In vs 1c the speaker describes his own psalm or singing
of the Lord as his work, ʿbdy, his labour, pwlhny; in vs 6 he
repeats these synonymous roots to describe pleonastically the
contents of his inspired speech or praise: God's work, ʿbd²,
and labour, pwlhn² in creation.[16]

Verse 7

The listing of the subject matter of the speaker's
inspired song or speech continues, though it is peculiar that

here the substantives have the object marker, the l, prefixed
to them, while the other substantives which we have interpreted as objects in vss 5c and 6 do not. In both vs 5c and
vs 6 the author pairs expressions which are basically synonymous, and so we would expect him to do the same in vs 7. The
phraseology of vs 7a is probably drawn from Ps 51, whereas,
that of 7b has no exact parallel in the Old Testament or
apocrypha. Given the preceding verse and vs 19, "the power of
His word" probably refers to the creative power of the word as
agent in creation,[17] but it is difficult to see in what sense
it can be regarded as synonymous with "the abundance of His
tenderness," unless the author simply wishes to say that both
are seen in the creative work of the Lord in creation.

Verse 8

    The instructional section of the Ode begins, as we noted,
with a repetition of "His word," mlth, the last word of vs 7b.
Thus, as the Ode presently stands, the didactic section is
formally linked with the preceding verses. The "I" of the
speaker disappears completely. Given what has come before it
and what follows in vss 10ff, we would have expected this
verse to continue with the theme of the Lord's creative
activity, but instead it takes up other activities associated
with the word, and does so in a reflective style quite unlike
the preceding verses.

    The verse has been variously rendered in the standard
translations. Charlesworth (71) suggests:

    For the Word of the Lord investigates that which is
                                              invisible,
    And reveals His thought.

Charlesworth vocalizes vs 8b wᵉdaglā mahšabteh, which, Brock
insists, should be rendered, "and deceives."[18] As Brock
points out, Charlesworth's translation supposes the vocaliza-
tion wad gālê, "and which reveals." Brock maintains that,

    Since, however, the antecedent is feminine, this
    translation is not possible, and it would seem
    better to analyze the verb as wᵉda-gᵉlê, 'and that
    which is revealed,' and to take the phrase as a
    further object of basyā, with mahšabteh as subject.

Brock's translation would read:

> For the word of the Lord investigates that which is
>   invisible,
> And His thought that which is revealed.

Brock's interpretation is, on the whole, more convincing than
that of Charlesworth, given the parallelism, and the good
sense it makes of the difficult Syriac of the verse.[19]

Commenting on the use of mlt² in Ode 41.14 Bauer (622)
says:

> Das syrische meltha ist, wo es sonst in den Oden
> auftritt (noch neunmal), das machtvolle Wort, mit
> dem Gott etwa die Schöpfung erstehen lässt oder
> seine Feinde niederestreckt. Nirgends hat es den
> Sinn von Logos (wie Joh 1.1).

While Bauer is correct in refusing simply to equate mlt² in
the Odes with the logos of Jn 1.1, he overstates his position,
for though "word" seems to be related to creation in Ode
16.7b, in vs 8 the word is involved neither in creation nor in
the defeat of God's enemies. With mlt² parallel to mhšbt²,
"thought," "will," "design," in vs 8b, the background for vs 8
is probably the notion that, as Wis 9.11 puts it, wisdom
"knows and understands all things." A claim is made in Wis
7.21-22 which seems to presuppose a notion of wisdom quite
similar to what we find in vs 8; Solomon declares that he has
learned "what is secret and what is manifest, for wisdom, the
fashioner of all things has taught me." See also Wis 8.4
which describes wisdom as an "initiate in the knowledge of
God" and as "an associate in his works."[20]

Verse 9

Verse 9 asserts that His works, ᶜbdwhy, and His thought,
mhšbth, ("His" referring back surely to the Lord) which the
Odist has been discussing, and which he now presents as
parallel, are not removed, at a distance from human beings,
but rather that they are within the range of human sight and
hearing. The combination of the eye seeing and the ear
hearing calls to mind the quotation in 1 Cor 2.9-10, which is
extant in neither the Old Testament nor the apocrypha:

What no eye has seen, nor ear heard, nor the heart
of man conceived, what God has prepared for those
who love him.

The same apocryphal text seems to underlie Gos.Thom. 17:

I shall give you that which eye has not seen, and
which ear has not heard, and which hand has not
touched and (which) has not arisen in the heart of
man.

Vs 9, however, lacks any note of "hiddenness and unveiling,"
which Conzelmann sees (the "widespread religious motif") as
the context for the text.[21]   In Ode 16.9 the "words" the eye
sees are not heavenly mysteries or realities suddenly made
manifest or revealed, but, given the use of "works" in this
Ode, probably the works of God in creation. It is not clear
how the ear hears "His thought"; perhaps the phrase is simply
added in the interest of parallelism, though it is naturally
suggested by the mention of the eye seeing. It would seem
that the "thought" or "design" referred to also is the thought
or design of God made manifest in the created world.[22]

Verses 10-12

    The verse begins with the third person masculine pronoun
hw, which Charlesworth insists, must refer back to "the Word"
(72, n.6).[23]   There is, however, the problem already mentioned
of the gender of mlt'.   The following vss suggests that the
subject is more likely the Lord, the antecedent, as well, of
the "His" in vs 9. In language inherited from the Old Testament the author confesses that the Lord is the creator of
earth and heaven, reversing the traditional order of creation
according to Genesis (see also Is 44.24). The bicola are
constructed in perfect parallelism, and the language can be
traced directly back to the Old Testament; for establishing a
place for the waters see Ps 104.9; Gen 1.9-10; Job 38.8-11;
Prov 8.29; for setting the stars in their places, see Ps
74.16, 148.6; Gen 1.14-19, and for stretching out the heavens,
see Ps 104.2. The image, however, of spreading wide or broad
the earth is peculiar to the Odist. Does the Odist perhaps
have some apologetic motive for mentioning the creation of the

earth first, for affirming that the Lord made the earth just
as He made the heavens? Gunkel contends: "Dieser Psalm kann
geradezu als eine Abkehr von der Lehre, dass die Welt böse und
nicht von Gott sei, aufgefasst werden."[24]

In vs 12a the author refers once again to the Lord's
creative activity in ordering and establishing creation, and
reports in vs 12b that the Lord rested from "His works,
ʿbdwhy, presumably the same works which "eye sees" according to
vs 9a.[25]

Verses 13-14

The work theme continues in vs 13, though it is no longer
the Lord who is subject, but rather created things. The Odist
shows his fondness for repeating sounds: he repeats the root
rht twice in vs 13a and ʿbd twice in vs 13b, vs 13b being in
complete parallelism with vs 13a. For created things to run
"their runnings," that is, their courses, is for them to "work
their works." Unlike God, however, they are not to cease from
their labours, for they are not equal to the Master of creation who can work and rest as He wishes. He alone fixed
creation and established it, and so created things follow His
dictates and designs. The divinely established order in
creation, with God as master, and the creation subject to Him,
is alluded to implicitly in vs 14. The Odist affirms that the
heavenly hosts are held firmly within the power and control of
God, that is, they are subject, mštʿbdyn, to His word, once
again the root ʿbd being used; here, however, in the eshtaphal, "made to work."

Scholars who have not recognized that vss 13ff form a
separate section of the Ode have sometimes seen in these
verses anti-sabbatical tendencies, which Harris and Mingana
(288) regard as "an unmistakable case of anti-Jewish polemic."
They believe that the Odist intends to ". . . say something
which shows that he does not mean to deduce the Jewish Sabbath
from the statements in Genesis."[26] The Odist, however, is
interested not in the question of sabbath rest but in God's
sovereignty as Creator; expressed by the fact that while God
rests, creation continues doing the work assigned to it.[27]

Verses 15-17

With our attention set on the heavenly luminaries in vs
14, the Odist draws our attention in vss 15-17 to the sun and
the night, to light and darkness. Harris and Mingana (286)
are disturbed that while the Odist ascribes to the sun the
rule over the day, he does not depict the moon as ruling the
night: "This is not in accordance with the book of Genesis.
There is, then, room for suspicion that the moon has been got
rid of by the Odist or lost from his text." As Emerton,
however, points out, the poet is using the image of a storehouse or treasury, symt', of light and darkness, and he could
scarcely have said that the moon is the storehouse of
darkness.[28]

Vs 16 begins with the verb ʿbd, which, we have seen, is
the unifying catchword of the Ode. If the form is taken as a
perfect, as the diacritical point in the manuscript indicates,
Emerton thinks that it must be taken as a reference "to the
single act of creation in the past, and that God, or His word
(see verses 5-6, 7, 8, 14) is the subject."[29] Emerton,
however, proposes an alternative:

> Perhaps it would be better to ignore the diacritical
> point, and vocalize the first verb as a participle,
> thus bringing the form into closer parallelism with
> the participle myt' in 16b, referring to night.[30]

As in vs 15, sun and night would parallel one another and be
the subjects of the verse. He also argues that ". . . the
lamadh at the beginning of 'day' in the first line would be
the sign of the direct object as it is before 'darkness' in
the parallel, and the difference in word order would not be a
serious difficulty."[31] The translation would then run:

> The sun, then, makes the day become bright;
> The night, then, brings darkness over the face of
>   the earth.

Since vss 15-17 are concerned with the activity or work of the
sun and the night, Emerton's proposal seems quite convincing.
Vss 15-17 demonstrate the truth of what is asserted in vs 13,
that created things, night and sun, do indeed run their course
and do their work, which is to make dark and to make bright,

without ceasing. This they do by constant "reception," which,
as Emerton suggests, ". . . probably refers to the fact that
sun and night succeed each other regularly: they 'take over
from each other' as we might say."[32]

Flemming (46), Ungnad and Staerk (18), Labourt and
Batiffol (17) all understand "their acceptance," qwblhwn, as
the subject of mmlyn in vs 17b, which is unlikely, since a
single subject does not normally stand with a plural participle. Emerton suggests, "Perhaps the first line is a nominal
clause, in which we supply the verb 'to be,' as often in
Syriac."[33] The participle, mmlyn from the root ml', "to
complete, fill, replenish, conclude; to be full, satisfied,"
has   caused   considerable   difficulty   for   translators.
Charlesworth (73) compares vs 17 with 1 Enoch 49.20 which
refers to the sun and moon completing their courses. Emerton,
however, points out that ". . . to complete one's course is
not   the   same   as   to   complete   God's   glory."[34] Harris and
Mingana (285), and many subsequent translators, emend mmlyn to
mmllyn, the pael participle of the verb ml, "to speak, say,
recite, talk," so that the line would read: "they tell of the
beauty of God." As support for the emendation Harris and
Mingana appeal to the similarity between this emended line and
Ps 19.1: "The heavens declare the glory of God."

Emerton captures the sense of vs 17: "In other words,
the sun and the night take over from each other every twenty-
four hours, and they take it in turns to proclaim God's
beauty."[35] In doing their assigned work, as described in vss
15-16, they proclaim God's glory; by the succession of day and
night, light and darkness, God's beauty is manifest and
proclaimed. Once again we find here the connection of work
and praise which is introduced in the very first line of the
Ode.

Verse 18

Charlesworth (73, n. 14) associates Ode 16.18 with Ode
1.1 and John 1.1-3. He sees a connection with Ode 1.1 because
of his translation of the Coptic, auo ntinarpefbol an as "And
I shall never be without Him." According to Crum, r bol or r

<u>pbol</u> means "become loosened, become free, hence, avoid, escape."[36] Thus Lattke (79) comes closer to the sense of the Coptic when he renders the line, "Und ich werde ihn nicht entfliehen." As for the alleged connection with Jn 1.1-3, it appears that the Odist makes no special effort to imitate the Johannine formulation, for in both the Peshitta and the Curetonian versions of Jn 1.3 the preposition that is used is <u>bl'd</u>, whereas in the Ode it is <u>lbd</u>. More importantly, in Jn 1.1-3 the subject is the Word who was from the beginning with God, whereas in Ode 16.18 it is the Lord Himself who is the subject. Jn 1.3 affirms that "all things were made through him, and without him was not anything made that was made." The <u>chōris</u> <u>autou</u>, "without him" refers to the fact that without the agency of the Word nothing that was created could have come into existence. Ode 16.18, on the other hand, states that nothing exists besides or outside of God, who is sovereign and eternal (18b-c), a claim that somewhat parallels 1QH X.9:

> and without Thee nothing is made,
> and nothing is known without Thy will.
> Except for Thyself, nothing exists, (10)
> and nothing is mighty beside Thee,
> and in the face of Thy glory nothing is,
> and Thy power is without price.

1QH VII:32:

> For Thou art a God of eternity
> and all Thy ways are established from everlasting
>   (32) to everlasting,
> and besides Thee there is nothing.
> How then is man, this nothing possessing but breath,
> to understand Thy marvelous deed (33) [unless Thou
>   t]e[a]ch [him]?

and 1QS XI.18:

> For without Thee no way is perfect,
> and without Thy will nothing is done.
> It is Thou who hast taught (18) all Knowledge,
> and all that is brought into being exists by Thy
>   will.
> And there is none other besides Thee
> to dispute Thy decision
> and to comprehend (19) all Thy holy Thoughts
> and to understand all Thy marvels and the power (20)
>   of Thy might.

Verse 19

According to this verse "the worlds," ʿlmᵓ, were made by
His word, and by the "thought of His heart" (see the parallel
use of these terms in vs 8). The plural of the word ʿlmᵓ,
like its Greek counterpart, aiōn, can mean "generations,"
"ages," "periods of time," but in the present context it
should probably be understood spatially, as "worlds," or
"spheres."[37]

Verse 20

Having affirmed that the whole cosmos is created by or
through the agency of God's word and the thought of His heart,
the Ode closes with a doxology in which the speaker offers
glory or praise, tšbwhtᵓ, to the Lord's name, just as in vs 5
he claims that the Spirit would speak the glory, tšbwhtᵓ, and
the beauty of the Lord when he opens his mouth.

Our discussion of the possible Sitz im Leben of the Ode
must take into consideration its structure. As we noted, the
Ode contains an "I" section in which the speaker reflects upon
his work, the singing of the Lord in His praises. The exact
nature of his work, unfortunately, remains unclear. The
second section, vss 8-20, is a didactic poem influenced
strongly by hymnic style. Neither section contains direct
address, plural imperatives, jussives which might indicate
that the Odist is directing his poem to an audience that is
present. Indeed, the concluding doxology in vs 20 is the only
piece of data which in itself would argue for a communal
context, for the didactic section contains no invitations, no
exhortations, offers no promises, incentives.

On the basis of the evidence culled from the Ode alone,
we cannot ascertain the Sitz im Leben, but major options are
available. First, we may consider the Ode to be a piece of
private devotional poetry composed by a person who considers
his life to be devoted to the praise of God. Vss 1-7 would,
in such a context, represent the author's personal reflections
on his work of praising, and vss 8-20, without any notable
sign of transition, without any normal introduction, would be

the speaker's meditative consideration of God's work in creation and creation's work and praise of God, concluding with an expression of praise.

A second possibility would be that the speaker possesses a special role as teacher/singer within the community. In vss 1-7 he recalls his calling and responsibility, and lays claim to the spirit's inspiration for what is to follow. Vss 1-7, then, could function as a preparatory narrative in which the speaker establishes his credentials for the teaching which he presents in vss 8-19, or 8-20, depending upon whether we take the doxology to be spoken by the teacher-singer, or as a response made by his audience. Aune, along with a number of other scholars, sees the speaker as a cultic prophet who operates within an early Christian worship setting, though there is no reason to assume a Christian origin and _Sitz im Leben_.[38] As Aune himself, however, notes, in the early Christian communities, ". . . every aspect of worship was regarded as a work of the Spirit of God. . . ."[39] James M. Robinson, similarly, explains the relationship of inspiration to prayer-language in Judaism and Early Christianity:

> Gebet und hymnisch gehobener Stil werden im Judentum und im Urchristentum nicht scharf voneinander getrennt. Vg. zu den Begriffen Act 16.25: proseuchomenoi hymnoun ton theon. Im allgemeinen wird man sagen können, dass die Gebete um so hymnischer werden, je enthusiastischer sie sind; denn das religiöse Lied hält man normalerweise für inspiriert. Nach Mc 12.36 sprach David den Ps 110 en pneumati hagiō. Wenn Zacharias das Benedictus anstimmt, heisst es Lc 1.67: eplēsthē pneumatos hagiou kai eprophēteusen . . . Tertullian Apol 30.4 beschreibt das christliche Gebet: sine monitore, quia de pectore oramus.[40]

Thus, a third option would be to see Ode 16.1-7 as the claim not of some official teacher, or designated leader, but the claim of an ordinary member of a worshiping group to the Spirit's inspiration for the message or teaching he or she has to present to the group in vss 8-19 or 20.[41]

CHAPTER IV

Ode 31

1. The abysses were melted from before the Lord,
   And darkness was destroyed by his appearance.

2. Error fell into error and perished because of him,
   And contempt received no part,
   And it sank by the truth of the Lord.

3. He opened his mouth and spoke grace and joy,
   And he spoke new praise to His name.

4. And he lifted his voice to the Most High,
   And he presented to Him those who had become sons
   through him.

5. And he was justified in His presence,
   Because so his Holy Father granted to him.

6. Come forth, you who were afflicted,
   And receive joy!

7. And take possession of yourselves through grace,
   And take for yourselves immortal life.

8. And they condemned me when I stood up,
   I, who had not been guilty.

9. And they divided my spoil,
   Though nothing was owed them.

10. But I endured and kept still and was silent,
    Like one who was not troubled by them.

11. Rather I stood unmoved like a firm rock,
    Which is whipped by the waves and endures.

12. And I bore their bitterness for the sake of humility,
    So that I might save my people and instruct it,

13. And that I might not render vain the promises to the
    patriarchs,
    To whom I promised the salvation of their seed.

Hallelujah!

Verses 1-2 describe in mythological language the defeat of the cosmological elements, "darkness" and "abysses," and of the "error" and "contempt," perhaps understood as hypostasized. Without any note of introduction vs 1 launches into a report of the event, describing it with perfect verbs, an ethpeel in vs 1a and an ethpaal in vs 1b. According to the phrase mn qdm in vs 1a, the abysses were dissolved "from before the Lord," though, as so frequently in the Odes, the identity of "the Lord," mry², is ambiguous. Paralleling mn qdm is the preposition mn in vs 1b, which should probably be interpreted as a preposition of agency or causality. The object of the preposition is hzwh, "his appearance," the third masculine singular suffix referring back to "the Lord." Vs 2 introduces "error" and "contempt" as subjects, and describes how they too were destroyed, using a pair of perfect verbs for each subject. In vs 2a the "perishing" is caused mnh, the third masculine singular object suffix having the Lord as its antecedent, and in 2c "sinking" is brought about mn šrrh dmry², "by the truth of the Lord." Vss 1-2 do not locate the defeats in any specific time or place. There is no indication that there is any battle involved; rather, according to vs 1, it is the appearance of the Lord which causes the collapse of the abysses and darkness.

Verses 3-5 report a series of events, whose connection with the preceding verses is unclear. The protagonist is "he," the third person singular masculine subject of the active perfect verbs in vss 3-4 and the subject of the ethpaal perfect verb in vs 5a. The identify of the subject can only be inferred from the actions which are predicated of him and the relationship implied by the description of the Most High as "his holy Father" in vs. 5. It is not clear how many different events are reported in these verses. Vs 3a can be interpreted to mean that "he" proclaimed or preached "grace and joy," or else it can be understood to stand in synonymous parallelism with vs 3b which refers to his speaking praise "to his name." The context for either or both actions is not given in the text. Vs 4a may be a repetition of vs 3b or may allude to yet another event. According to vs 4b the subject delivers over to "him," presumably the Most High mentioned in vs 4a, "those who had become sons through him." The section concludes with the report that the protagonist was "justified," ˒zddq, "in his presence," bprswph, that is, before the Most High, and vs 5b explains that the justification took place because his holy Father granted or appointed it.

It is probable that the protagonist of the events reported in vss 3-5 is to be identified with "the Lord" whose presence occasions the destruction described in vss 1-2.

Verses 6-7 represent an address, using a series of four plural imperatives. Those addressed are described in vs 6a as "you who were afflicted," but no indication is given of the identity of the speaker, of those addressed, or of the setting for the address.

Verses 8-13 are a narrative spoken by the first person singular in which the speaker recounts with perfect verbs the events surrounding his persecution. The speaker does not specifically identify himself, nor does he address a specific audience. He stresses his silent endurance (vss 10-12a), his innocence (vss 8-9) and in vss 12b-13 explains his motives: to save his people and to instruct it, so as not to negate the promises he made to the patriarchs to save their seed.

The modern interpreter of the Odes faces serious difficulties when he approaches Ode 31, not least of all because of the transitions in form and content in the Ode. In his study of Ode 31 Kittel remarks:

> Gerade hier ist einmal sehr deutlich zu verfolgen, wie der Dichter es verschmäht, durch Andeutung einer Überleitung dem Leser oder Hörer das Verständnis der Übergänge zu erleichtern.[1]

This particular aspect of the Odist's style deserves more study, but in any case, it is such a constant feature of the style of the Odes that it cannot be explained away as carelessness or inadvertence. We must presume that whether the Ode was intended to be read or spoken in public, or whether it is an exercise of private devotion, the author knew what he wanted to say and how to say it. If it was written or addressed to an audience, we must presume that the audience

would know how to understand the persons and events he alludes
to and the forms he uses in an unambiguous way. The language
of the Ode must have made immediate sense for those who shared
the cultural background and the theological assumptions of the
author. It is the task of the interpreter to endeavor to
discover the associations, the formal and religious schemata
which readers or listeners would have brought to the text in
order to understand it.[2]

Verse 1

In the cosmological scheme of the Old Testament the
abysses, thwm' (thwm in Hebrew, abyssos in Greek), stand for
the subterranean sea, the symbol of chaos and disorder, the
original flood or floods of water (Gen 1.2ff).[3] By extension
the term can also refer to the underworld as a place of
imprisonment (Ps 107.26; Lk 8.31; Rev 9.1, 11.7, 17.18,
20.1,2) or the abode of the dead (Ps 71.20; Rom 10.7).
Abysses are paralleled in vs 1b by "darkness," hšwk', which in
Gen 1.2 is also used to characterize the primal chaos: ". . .
and darkness was upon the face of the abyss."[4] Like "abysses"
it can also allude to the underworld (Jb 10.21, 17.13; Mt
8.12, 22.13, 25.30; 2 Pet 2.17). Conzelmann remarks, "Cosmo-
logically the idea of the underworld merges into that of the
ocean depths; both are dark spheres of non-being."[5] "Darkness," of course, also is associated with anything evil or
threatening, e.g., captivity (Ps 107.10), wickedness (Ps
74.20; 82.5).[6] In Ode 31 the parallel terms abysses and
darkness can refer, then, either to the primitive chaos or to
the underworld seen as the abode of the dead. It is also
possible that for the Odist the distinction between the
underworld and the world has disappeared, as is obviously the
case, for example, in gnostic myth.[7]

The verb used to describe the destruction of the abysses
in vs 1a is 'tpšrw, the ethpeel of pšr, "to melt, be melted."
The image implied by the verb is probably that of wax melting,
a figure used frequently in descriptions of theophanies in the
Old Testament and in the pseudepigrapha (Ps 97.5; Mic 1.4; Jdt
16.15; 1 Enoch 1.6).[8] In 4 Ezra 13.4, theophanic features,

melting among them, are used in describing the coming or
appearance of "the man" from the sea, whose attributes and
functions parallel those elsewhere ascribed to the Messiah in
this 1 century C.E. apocalypse.[9] Verse 1, then, seems to
report the effects of the "Lord's" coming or appearance,
though it is not clear who is being referred to by the title
"Lord," God Himself, or some other figure.[10] In any case he
is of such stature or importance in the eyes of the Odist that
his appearance can be described in terms traditionally associated with an epiphany of God Himself.

Verse 2

This verse closely parallels verse 1; "error," t‘ywt’,
which parallels "abysses," perished because of him, just as
abysses melted from before the Lord. As darkness was destroyed by his presence in vs 1b, so "contempt," šytwta’, sank
by the truth of the Lord in vs 2b. In addition to the cosmological elements of chaos or the underworld, the coming or
appearance of the Lord, described as "the truth of the Lord,"
that is, the Lord in his quality of truth or in his office of
truth-bringer, brings about the destruction of error and
contempt. The author uses ironic language to depict their
destruction: error, which presumably leads astray, itself
errs and perishes. Vs 2b has found no universally accepted
interpretation, but it seems to mean that contempt likewise
lost its way and consequently sank. Perhaps the verb tb’y,
"to sink, to be sunk, swallowed up," alludes to the flood
story, in which case the appearance of the Lord signals
judgement and punishment.

The question of the precise meanings of "error" and
"contempt" remains unresolved. "Contempt" is particularly
troublesome, but whatever it signifies, it parallels, is
perhaps synonymous with, "error," and further, it is destroyed
by the "truth of the Lord."[11]

Verse 3

As we noted, the identity of the third person masculine
singular subject of the perfect verbs in this verse is

uncertain, and the structure of the verse itself is ambiguous.
Gunkel proposes reading vss 3-4 as three bicola:

> 3. Da öffnete er seinen Mund
>   und verkündete Gnade und Freude,
>   Er sang ein neues Lied seinem Namen,
> 4.   und erhob seine Stimme zum Höchsten.
>   Er brachte ihn dar die Söhne
>   die in seinen Händen waren.[12]

If Gunkel's analysis is correct, and the clear and strong
parallelism that his arrangement yields is a forceful argument
in its favor, the first bicolon, vs 3a in our enumeration,
would describe the subject's speaking, perhaps in the sense of
preaching or proclamation, to an unspecified audience. The
second bicolon, vss 3b-4a, would refer to the subject's praise
offered to the Most High, the masculine singular suffix in
lšmh in vs 3b anticipating the "Most High" in vs 4a.

Aune understands the "joy," hdwt², which the subject
speaks to be the joy associated in the Jewish tradition with
eschatological salvation.[13]   Indeed, Jewish and Christian
texts abound which depict the eschatological age as a time of
overwhelming joy and gladness.[14]   Joy, however, also plays an
important role in Hermetic literature, and in some mystery
religions; Conzelmann even calls it "a basic mood in mystery
piety."[15]   For Philo joy is the result of mystical union with
God,[16] and for the gnostic it is saving knowledge which brings
him or her joy and peace.[17]

The term "grace," tybwt², equivalent to the Greek charis
and the Hebrew hnn or hsd, has a wide range of meanings.   In
the Old Testament hsd is above all God's kindness and mercy in
joining Israel to himself in a covenant, though it is also
seen in God's answering of prayers, His redeeming, forgiving,
giving life, saving from death and sickness.[18]   In the Qumran
community it is above all the covenantal notion of "grace"
which dominates: the sectarians regarded themselves as a
community founded on God's covenant of hsd.   The term charis
appears 25 times in Lk and Acts, only once in Jn, in Jn 1.14,
and is Paul's preferred way of speaking of God's gift in
salvation.[19]

When the speaker in vs 3a speaks of "grace and joy" he is
probably talking about God's gift or favor of salvation and
the joy that comes from it. Whether it recalls some special
or particular divine intervention, heralds its presence, or
predicts its future coming, is not clear. That the Odist uses
"grace" and "joy" as connoting salvation seems evident from
his use of them in the address in vss 6-7, where "joy" is
offered to the afflicted, and "grace" is the means by which
they can take possession of themselves and get immortal life.

To speak "new praise," or "new hymn," tsbhwt' hdt', is an
expression which is relatively common in the Old Testament and
seems to mean simply giving praise or glory to God.[20]

Verse 4

As we suggested, we should, on the basis of its parallelism of structure with vs 3b, regard vs 4a as a reference to
the figure's praising the Most High, or we should couple it
with the presentation of those who had become sons, mentioned
in vs 4b, so that it would refer to some aspect of the presentation. For the reasons noted above, the first seems the
better option.

Who are "those who have become sons through him" and who
is the "him," object of "through"?[21] Jewish apocalyptic
looked forward to the renewal of Israel's covenantal relationship with God, whereby Israel's filial relationship with God
would be restored (Jub 1.15ff; Ps Sol 17.27; Wis 5.5; 1 Enoch
72.1).[22] The Qumran sectarians claimed to be living in the
age to come and thought of themselves as already enjoying the
eschatological status of "sons,"[23] and early Christians
frequently described themselves as children or sons of God and
claimed to have received life from God.[24] In his commentary
on Jn 1.14 Bultmann stresses the eschatological character of
sonship in the religious literature of the period of the New
Testament:

> Vor allem wird der Gedanke der Gotteskindschaft des
> Menschen zu einem "eschatologischen" Begriff, sowohl
> im Judentum wie in den Mysterienreligionen: Gottes
> Kind (oder Sohn) ist der Mensch, dann, wenn er in
> eine neue Existenz versetzt wird, sei es am Ende des

jetzigen Äon, wenn Gott die Welt erneuert, sei es
schon jetzt, dadurch dass der Mensch durch die Weihe
des Mysteriums zum Sohne Gottes gemacht, neu
"gezeugt" oder "geboren" wird.[25]

From the perfect verbs in Ode 31.4b it is clear that
"they have already become sons," that is, are already in
possession of eschatological salvation; they have already been
brought into the filial relationship with God. How this has
been achieved is not clear from the context, though perhaps
there is some connection with the preaching or proclamation
alluded to in vs 3a. It is also noteworthy that in vs 7
"grace" is associated with taking "immortal life." Is there
some implied connection between "becoming sons" and taking
immortal life?

The sense of qrb, the pael perfect of the verb "to bring,
lay near, to offer, to present," seems to be that the subject
leads those who have become sons, he brings them near to the
Most High, he brings them into the divine presence.[26]

Verse 5

The report which extends from vs 3, or perhaps from vs 1,
climaxes in this verse, and consists in the "justification" of
the figure who has proclaimed grace and joy (vs 3a), who
praises the Most High (vs 3b-4a) and who presented those who
had become sons to the Most High. The Syriac of vs 5a, as it
stands, is meaningless, for prsph cannot really be construed
as "himself," as most translators understand it.[27] It seems
best to follow J. Strugnell's suggestion and insert the
preposition b before the substantive, giving us the phrase "in
his presence," that is, in the presence of the Most High, to
whom in vs 4b the subject had already brought near the new
sons.[28]

Vs 5b adds the important note that he was justified
because so "his holy Father" granted or ordained. Vs 5b,
then, implies that the figure is himself a son of "his holy
Father," so that what others become, perhaps through him, he
himself already is.[29] Secondly, the Most High is described

not simply as "Father," but as his "holy Father," a feature
which J.-E. Menard regards as a sign of the Ode's affinity
with New Testament and biblical tradition, rather than with
gnosticism, stoicism or hermeticism, which use "Father" in the
absolute form.[30]

The classical commentaries on the Odes are divided in
their interpretation of "was justified," ᵓ zddq.[31] Most
translators and commentators seek help in interpreting this
verse from 1 Tim 3.16, probably a fragment of a hymn:[32]

> Who was manifested in the flesh,
> vindicated, edikaiōthē, in the spirit,
> seen by angels,
> preached among the nations,
> believed on in the world,
> taken up in glory.

Martin Dibelius and Hans Conzelmann interpret edikaiōthē en
pneumati as ". . . clearly a paraphrase for the exaltation
into the sphere of the 'spirit' (pneuma), as is indicated in a
very similar manner in Rom 1:4."[33] Unlike Paul's use of the
term, in 1 Tim it refers "to the entrance into the divine
realm, the realm of 'righteousness' (dikaiosunē)," in the
sense in which it can also be found in Corp Herm 13.9.[34] Thus
Dibelius and Conzelmann interpret Ode 31.5 to mean that the
victory of the redeemer figure is signaled by his being
designated as vindicated or justified.[35] Reginald Fuller is
convinced by the use of phrases such as "in glory," "in the
spirit," and "seen by angels" that the author of the hymnic
fragment has as his model some form of cosmic coronation
ceremony, and so understands "vindication" here not as an
attestation of the justice of Christ in his resurrection into
glory, but as "the exaltation in language reminiscent of
earlier Jewish Hellenistic Christology (Rom 1.4)."[36] The
justification or vindication in Ode 31.5a, then, seems to
refer to the exaltation into the divine presence of a figure,
probably a saviour figure. Nothing in the Ode up to this
point, however, justifies identifying the figure with
Christ.[37]

Verses 6-7

The four plural imperatives demand a subject, but none is
provided in the text. Perhaps the speaker of the poem, who
has remained completely in the background, is the speaker of
these imperatives. Perhaps we are to understand that the
figure who is the subject of vss 1-5 speaks these verses. It
could be that vss 6-7 are a sample of the sort of speech
referred to in vs 3a, for, as we noted, the objects of the
speech, "grace and joy" are repeated in these verses. In any
case, the placement of these verses and their lack of introduction are puzzling.

It is not clear from where "the afflicted" are to "come
forth." When they are admonished to "receive joy" they are
being invited to make their own the state of salvation characterized by joy, or perhaps just to hear and receive the joyful
news of salvation. To "take possession of yourselves" is
parallel to "take for yourselves immortal life" and should be
understood accordingly as to take possession of the immortal
life which is offered them. Unfortunately, "joy," "grace,"
and "immortal life" all refer to salvation in such a wide
variety of religious systems that it is impossible to use them
to pin down the precise religious and cultural context of the
Ode. Scholars who see in vss 6-7 an allusion to Christ's call
to those imprisoned in the underworld go far beyond the evidence afforded by this Ode.[38]

Verses 8-9

Without preparation or introduction a speaker appears,
for vss 8-9 begin a narrative section spoken in the first
person singular. The subject of vss 8-9 is in the third
person masculine plural. Formally the Odist stresses the
unity of thought of these two lines by his use of the root
ḥyb: in vs 8a, wḥybwny, "and they condemned me," in vs 8b
mḥyb , "guilty," and in vs 9b mtthyb, "owed," and by the
parallelism of thought between 8a and 9a, and 8b and 9b. The
first line of each bicolon reports the activity of the speaker's persecutors, while the second underlines his innocence.
Most commentators recognize in vs 9a echoes of Ps 22.18:

". . . they divide my garments among them, and for my raiment
they cast lots," the passage that surely also played a role in
the shaping of the passion narratives of the canonical
gospels (Mt 17.35; Mk 15.24; Lk 23.34; Jn 19.24).

Verses 10-11

The use of the root sbr in the paʿel perfect in vs 10a,
and repeated as the paʿel active participle in vs 11b, makes
it clear that the endurance of the speaker is the major point
of these two lines. The use of the first person singular
pronoun followed by dyn underscores the contrast that is drawn
between the silent endurance of the speaker and the unjust
treatment meted out to him. The synonymous expressions štqt,
"I kept still," and šlyt, "I was silent," a poetic hendiadys,
gives special emphasis to the speaker's silence during his
persecution. As background for these verses Is 53.7 comes
immediately to mind. The New Testament writers also make use
of this motif in describing the stance of Jesus during his
passion.[39] The verb in vs 10b, ʾttzyʿ, could be analyzed as a
first person singular future, which, with ʾyk dlʾ, would mean
"in order that I might not be troubled," or as a third person
masculine singular perfect, "like one who was not troubled."
It seems better to understand the verb as in the perfect and
the resultant meaning corresponds admirably with the simile
which follows in Vs 11.

Verse 11a parallels vs 19a; the speaker is silent and
unmoved, motionless as a solid rock. The Syriac of vs 11b is
difficult to understand, but whatever the exact translation,
the general sense is clear enough: the speaker stood like a
solid rock that is unmoved, by "columns of waves"
(Charlesworth, 117), "Brecher" (Lattke, 165), "väldiga vågor"
(Beskow and Hidal, 48).[40] The formulation may have been
inspired not only by Is 53 and perhaps Is 50.7, but also, as
Gunkel suggests, by the Greek stoic ideal.[41] See, for example, Marcus Aurelius, Med IV.49 in which the author compares
himself to a promontory that is unmoved by the fury of the
waves which dash against it.

It is difficult to know how to construe vs 10b. Does the author intend to say that, though persecuted, the speaker was really not troubled by his enemies? Is there, then, a hint that he only _seems_ to be oppressed, but is really unaffected by all that is done to him? In the _Gospel of Peter_, a document which is commonly recognized as exhibiting docetic tendencies, we find phraseology similar to Ode 31.10:

> And they brought out two malefactors and crucified the Lord in the midst between them. But he held his peace, as if he felt no pain.[42]

Whether or not Ode 31.10 or the Gospel of Peter is "docetic," they both seem to be dependent upon a tradition which depicts a man who silently endures, as if he feels no pain, is not troubled.

The Odist is probably inspired in the narrative in vss 8-12a by the tradition of the persecution and exaltation of the innocent just man which was a part of the Jewish wisdom tradition, and which doubtless also shaped the canonical Gospels' passion accounts.[43] George W. E. Nickelsburg surveys the various wisdom tales of the persecution and vindication of the just man, and, of all those he analyzes, the Ode seems closest to Wis 2.12ff.[44] In Wis 2 the ungodly lie in wait against the just man because "he is inconvenient to us and opposes our actions," because he claims to have knowledge of God, and claims God as his father (see Ode 31.5b). In their plan, his death will test the validity of his claims and the accusations he makes against them. As Nickelsburg notes, "the last line suggests that the ungodly have in mind a formal legal condemnation" (see Ode 31.8a).[45]

A second scene runs from Wis 4.20-5.14 and is characterized by Nickelsburg as "a post-mortem confrontation between the righteous man and his persecutors."[46] In this second scene the primary point is the exaltation and the acclamation of the just man. The truth of his claim, for example, to be God's son, is validated in his exaltation to the heavenly court in Wis 5.5. His persecutors are forced to acknowledge his exalted status. Nickelsburg observes that the author anticipates the outcome of the second scene in his editorial section, where he refutes the views of the wicked, Wis 2.21-3.10.[47] This section already gives the author's answer to the problem of the persecution of the just man: though he appears to the wicked to have died, he is enjoying immortality, he is at rest, and is a member of the heavenly court. Though there is a reference to the juridical function of the exalted just man as judge of his opponents (3.8), it receives no special emphasis, because, as Nickelsburg recognizes,

> . . . exaltation is in the service of vindication.
> The author is mainly interested in showing that what
> the righteous claimed was true, and that what the
> ungodly said was false.[48]

For Wis the exaltation of the just man is synonymous with his being translated, taken up into heaven and being made a member of the divine court. Again Nickelsburg: ". . . there is a sense in which there is an identity or at least continuity between death and exaltation . . . the righteous man's persecution and death are the cause of his exaltation."[49] Dieter Georgi goes a step further in his interpretation, suggesting that the reality of death and suffering is denied in the case of the persecuted just man:

> Genau gesehen hat der Weg des Gerechten nur den
> Schein des Leidens und Sterbens. Es wird mit
> Absicht doketisch geredet . . . Es verhält sich mit
> dem Gerechten nicht so, wie die Gottlosen in ihrer
> Verblendung meinen. Was die Gottlosen zu sehen
> glauben, ist keine Wirklichkeit. Das Leiden des
> Gerechten geschieht nur dem Augenschein nach.
> Selbst sein Tod ist nur Schein.[50]

As for the death of the just man, Georgi claims that according to Wis,

> Der Gerechte ist nicht gestorben, sondern das, was
> als sein Tod erscheint, ist in Wirklichkeit seine
> Entrückung, und seine Entrückung ist gleichbedeutend
> mit seiner Erhöhung in richterliche und königliche
> Würde und Funktion.[51]

If, indeed, there is a docetic sense implied in Ode 31.10b, it can probably be traced back to the docetism which Georgi sees in the Wisdom tradition.

Verses 12-13

The motif of the persecuted just man continues in vs 12a. Perhaps "their bitterness," mryrwthwn, which the speaker bore, is inspired by Ps 69:21: "They gave me poison for food, and for my thirst they gave me vinegar (mrr² in the Peshitta) to drink," where the offering of vinegar or sour wine is a hostile gesture expressive of the hatred of the psalmist's enemies. The Psalm is alluded to in all the canonical Gospels' passion narrative, in GosPet.,[52] and is also used by the Qumran psalmist in 1QH 4.11.[53] The simple phrase "for the sake of humility," mtl mkykwt², is also rooted in the tradition of the innocent man who endures persecution.[54] In vss 12b-13 the speaker explains his purpose and intent in enduring his persecution: to "save my people and instruct it," according to vs 12b, mtl d²prwq l⁵my w²rtywhy. G. J. Reinink judges that it is better to understand ²rtywhy as derived from the root yrt, "to inherit" rather than from rt², "to instruct," ". . . weil, das Erbe des Volkes besser zum Kontext passt, wo von den Verheissungen an die Erzväter die Rede ist."[55] Brien McNeil, however, maintains that the two verbs in vs 12b form a hendiadys, so that redemption is depicted as consisting in the instruction of the speaker's people.[56] If McNeil is correct, the instruction which saves is centered on mkykwth, the humility the speaker showed in his silent endurance of persecution.

In vs 13 the humble endurance of the speaker is connected with the promises to the patriarchs, and in vs 13b the speaker announces that the promises alluded to in vs 13a are what he himself promised, and have as their content the salvation of the patriarchs' seed.[57] Not only, then, does the speaker depict his work as effecting the salvation promised to the patriarchs and their posterity, but he identifies himself as the very one who made the promise. In the Old Testament it is God Himself who made the promises to the patriarchs (Mic 7.20; Gen 17.7, 18.18, 22.17; 2 Sam 7.11-16; see also Lk 1.55).

There are at least three sections to this Ode, perhaps four. Vss 1-2 describe in language approximating that of a

theophany, the impact of the "Lord's" appearance on the
underworld (vs 1) and upon error and contempt (vs 2). Vss 3-5
report the events of his preaching (vs 3a), his praise of the
Most High (vss 3b-4a), and his bringing near to the Most High
the new sons, probably a term for the "saved" (vs 4b), and his
own vindication in the divine presence (vs 5). We can regard
vss 1-5 as unified by the notion of "appearance," though it is
used only in vs 1b; for the section begins with a report of
the Lord's appearance before abysses, darkness, error and
contempt, and ends with his appearance before the divine
presence with the "sons," and his own justification before
God, his Holy Father.

Vss 6-7 do not seem to fit in their present place in the
Ode. If they are understood as spoken by the "he" who is
subject of vss 1-5, it is certainly not clearly indicated, and
the verses badly placed. The section 1-5 ends formally and
thematically with the vindication of the figure. The address
gives the impression of having been tacked on; perhaps it was
a fragment which once belonged in the body of the text, for
example, after vs 3a, or it may have been added as a sample of
the sort of speech the figure made.

Vss 8-13 are formally and thematically different from vss
1-5 and vss 6-7. If vss 1-5 and vss 8-13 appeared as two
separate poems, we would have no reason to think they were
referring to the same figure, though in their present context,
presumably the "he" whose activities and vindication are
reported in 1-5 is the same person as the "I" who speaks in
vss 8-13. The "I" is the persecuted righteous man, whose
vindication, oddly, is not mentioned, but probably presupposed
as already having taken place. As the Ode presently stands,
vss 8-13 appear to be the speech of the figure whose vindication is reported in vs 5. So vindicated, he reports his
endurance through persecution, and in vss 12b-13 presents his
motives for submitting himself to persecution. It is likely
that vss 8-13 originally belonged in another context, and were
only later added to vss 1-7.

There are, however, certain bases for bringing the two
figures together. As we noted, vs 13 applies to the figure

language used of activities of the God of the Old Testament, and vss 1-2 also do so implicitly. The figures are saviour figures, clearly so in vss 12b-13, and also in vs 4b if we take the "through him" to refer to the subject; the figure in vs 3 is probably a preacher, and in vs 12b "I" is one who instructs. Apparently these similarities were sufficient for the poet to warrant bringing the two sections together. Moreover, it is possible that both were, from the start, written about the same saviour figure, but originally used in different contexts, employing different poetic expressions and dependent upon different theological traditions.

Because we are unable at this stage of our research to answer satisfactorily the questions posed by the peculiar changes of form and content, we are unable to address the problem of the Sitz im Leben of the poem in its final form.

CHAPTER V

Ode 33

1. Then grace again ran and expelled corruption,
   and descended into it in order to lay it waste.

2. And he had brought about complete destruction from before
   him,
   And he had corrupted all his works.

3. And he stood upon a high peak and let his voice go forth
   From (one) end of the earth to the (other) end of it.

4. And he drew to him(self) all those who listened to him,
   For he did not appear as evil.

5. But the perfect virgin rose up,
   Who was proclaiming and inviting and speaking:

6. Sons of men, turn back!
   And their daughters, come!

7. Leave behind the ways of that corruption,
   And approach me!

8. And I will enter into you,
   And I will bring you forth from destruction,
   And I will make you wise in the ways of truth.

9. You will not be corrupted,
   Nor will you be destroyed.

10. Listen to me and be saved,
    For the grace of God I am speaking among you,

11. And by my hand you will be saved, and you will become
    blessed.
    Your judge I am,

12. And those who have put me on will not be deprived,
    But will possess incorruption in the new age/world.

13. My elect, walk in me!
     And my ways I will make known to them who desire me,
     And I will promise them my name.

Hallelujah!

Verse 1 reports with three perfect verbs the activity of "grace," tybwt', and in a subordinate clause in vs 1b explains the motive for the descent mentioned in the same line. It is not clear who or what is the antecedent of the masculine singular third person object suffix attached to the preposition b in vs 1b, but the nearest singular masculine substantive is hbl', either "corruption" (or "corruptor"). The relationship of vs 1b to vs 1a is ambiguous owing to the variety of possible meanings of the conjunction w which introduces vs 1b. We could understand vs 1b as an event which followed the action reported in vs 1a, or we could regard it as in more or less synonymous parallelism with vs 1a.

There is a shift of subject in vs 2; the perfect verbs here and in vss 3-4 demand a masculine singular subject. Once again, the only possible antecedent mentioned in the text is hbl'. The identification of corruption as subject is made virtually certain by vs 2b which reports that the subject "corrupted" or "ravaged," hbl. Vss 3-4 report that a masculine singular subject spoke and drew listeners to himself. It is not certain that the subject of vss 3-4 is the same as that of vs 2, but it is likely, since there is no indication that a new subject has been introduced. If vss 2-4 describe the actions of a single subject, then perhaps the corruption and destruction referred to in vs 2 is effected by, or is the result of, the speech mentioned in vss 3-4. Vs 4b both characterizes the speaker and offers an explanation for his success in drawing listeners to himself: he is evil, but he did not appear as such.

Verse 5 continues as a report, but now the subject is "the perfect virgin" whose activities closely parallel but actually are antithetical to those of the subject of vss 3-4. As he "stood up," qm (vs 3a), so she "rose up," qmt, and as he "let his voice go forth" (vs 3a), so she "was proclaiming and inviting and speaking."

Verses 6-13 provide us with the speech of the perfect virgin, a speech, which, we shall see, resembles a typical Hellenistic religious Propagandarede, studied so successfully by Eduard Norden.[1] The speech of the perfect virgin can be broken down into the following elements:

a.) Address and Imperatives: vss 6-7

The two bicola, each containing two plural imperatives,
are in parallelism with one another. Those addressed are
identified in vs 6.

b.) Motives: vss 8-9

1. Verse 8 is a promise spoken by the "I" of the speaker
to "you" plural. The verbs of this tricolon are all
imperfect.

2. Verse 9 is also a promise, but the subject of the
imperfect verbs in this bicolon is the "you" plural
of those addressed.

a'.) Imperatives: vs 10a

The line presents a pair of plural imperatives, perhaps
to be understood as a hendiadys.

b'.) Motives: vss 10b-12

1. Verse 10b is an "I" statement, probably an
identification, directed to "you" plural. It
provides the grounds for the exhortation in vs 10a.

2. Verse 11a is a set of two promises, with "you" plural
as the subject of the imperfect verbs.

3. Verse 11b, like vs 10b, is formulated in the
"I-style" and directed to "you" plural. Here the
revelation of the identity of the speaker provides
the basis for the promise formulated in vs 11a.

4. Verse 12, like vss 8,9 and 11a, is a promise, but it
is phrased in a generalized form. The plural subject
of the two imperfect verbs are "those," hnwn, who are
the subject of the perfect verb in the subordinate
clause introduced by d.

a.'') Imperative: vs 13a

The perfect virgin's listeners are addressed directly as
"my elect," and they are the subject of the imperative
in this line.

b.'') Motives: vs 13b-c

The motive for responding to the exhortation or command
in vs 13a is the promise formulated by the speaker in a
pair of first person imperfect verbs. The indirect

objects of both verbs are identified, as in verse 12, by
hnwn plus the subordinate clause introduced by d. Thus,
the speaker's promise is again in a generalized form.
Verse 13 provides a fitting conclusion to the speech, the
imperative of vs 13a, "walk with/in me," reiterating the
imperatives of vss 6b and 7b: "come," and "approach me," and
the promise of vs 13b "my ways I will make known," corresponding to the promise of vs 8b: "I will make you wise in the
ways of truth."

The speech in vss 6-13 sets up a deliberate contrast
between the speaker and the figure described in vss 2-4.
According to vs 7 those addressed are exhorted to leave the
ways of "that corruption," hbl' hn' and to approach the
speaker, the perfect virgin. The perfect virgin promises in
vs 8b to bring forth those whom she calls "from destruction,"
mn 'bdn', repeating the root used in vs 2b to describe the
activity of "corruption," w'wbd l' bdn'. The parallel promise
in vs 9 repeats the same roots: "you will not be corrupted,"
l' tthblwn, and "you will not be destroyed," l' t' bdwn. In vs
12b the perfect virgin promises "incorruption" in the new age,
l' hbl'. It is, then, precisely corruption and the destruction which he causes which the perfect virgin calls her
hearers to leave, and what she offers them is exactly the
opposite of corruption of his destruction.

According to vs 4 corruption is successful, for his voice
extended throughout the earth and he attracted listeners to
himself, though he is, according to vs 2, the one who destroys
and corrupts. The perfect virgin, in the context of this Ode,
is a late-comer; she has to call her hearers away from her
rival, whom she characterizes as "corruption" in vs 7a. As
motivation for conversion from her opponent she offers not
only promises, but identifies herself in "I-style" statements
as the judge of her listeners (vs 11), and, depending upon how
we construe vs 10b, either as the one who speaks the grace of
God, or as the grace of God itself.

If we understand vs 10b as the perfect virgin's identification of herself as the grace of God, then it is simple to
see how vs 1 serves as an introduction to the whole of the

Ode. Grace descends into corruption or into its realm to lay
it waste and it does so by taking away from it those whom it
had drawn into its destructive power.

Verse 1

The language of this verse presents a number of difficult
problems. The conjunction dyn stands as the second word of
the line. Unless the original first verses of the Ode are
missing from the text as we presently have it, we cannot
regard the conjunction as a connective. Moreover, the word
occurs in exactly the same position in Ode 17, which otherwise
shows no sign of being incomplete at the beginning. Both in
Ode 33 and in Ode 17 it is probably best to translate dyn as
"then," in the sense of a fixed point in time.

The third word of the first line is twb, "again, yet,
too; at last; otherwise; besides" (Costaz, 388), which Bauer
(613) refers to as "das im Grunde beziehungslose 'wiederum'."[2]
The first few words of the line lead Harris and Mingana to
observe: "This Ode seems to begin abruptly and unintelli-
gibly; we suggest that something has been lost at the beginning" (376).[3] Harris and Mingana are perhaps a bit too rash;
we need not presume that the original lines of the Ode have
been lost, if we take twb as "again" and understand it as
Gressmann (465) does: Grace ". . . widerholt was sie schon
oft getan hat."

The subject of vs 1, tybwt', "grace, graciousness, kindness, goodness," carries a wide variety of meanings in the
Odes, depending upon the context in which it is found. In Ode
33 it is quite clearly an hypostatized figure,[4] as is its
opponent, "corruption," hbl'. Why grace is depicted as having
"run" or having "made rapid progress," rhtt, is far from
evident, and the meaning of the second verb in vs 1a, šbqt, is
uncertain.[5] Šbqt can be translated as "dismissed"
(Charlesworth, 120), "hat verlassen" (Lattke, 165), "stötte
bort" (Beskow and Hidal, 46), but Bauer (613) gives what is
probably the best translation for this context: "vertrieb."
Since, according to vs 1b, grace descended in order to lay it
(presumably "corruption") waste, it makes the best sense to

understand grace driving corruption away, banishing it,
expelling it. Since it is stated that grace "descended,"
nhtt, it appears that grace originates from above, perhaps
from the heavens, though it is also possible that the descent
is from earth into the underworld, also a fitting place for an
encounter with corruption. The prepositional phrase in vs 1b,
bh has been variously construed by the commentators, but the
masculine singular object pronoun probably refers back to
"corruption."[6]

Verse 2

As we noted, the perfect verbs in vs 2, as well as those
in vss 3-4, require a third person masculine singular subject.
It seems likely that the figure who destroys in vs 2 is the
same one who is described as speaking and attracting listeners
in vss 3-4. Many commentators see grace, or Christ, or some
saviour figure, as the subject of vss 2-4,[7] but there are
three problems with such an interpretation:

1. The change in gender in vs 2 and vss 3-4 argues
   against seeing grace as the subject of vss 3-4.
2. Vs 4b indicates clearly that the figure who spoke and
   succeeded in drawing listeners did so because he did
   not appear as he truly was, "evil," byš'.
3. Vs 2b describes the figure's activity as "corrupting," hbl, using the same root that is found in the
   name of grace's opponent, hbl'.

As a general principle, when we have a masculine singular noun
appearing in the preceding verse, we should regard it as the
most likely subject of verbs which demand a masculine singular
subject, providing that makes sense in the context, and
indeed, seeing corruption as the subject makes far better
sense than the convoluted explanations and solutions of
despair posited by most commentators.

Reinink presents an interesting variation on the interpretation of vss 2-4 as the work of a saviour figure. He contends that the subject of vss 2-4 must be corruption, but
suggests that corruption parodies the work of the saviour:
". . . das Verderben verfuhr wie z.B. der Erlöser handeln

würde, indem es, die Vernichtung vernichtete, und wird als der
grosse Betrüger geschildert (vgl. zum Thema des Nachahmung des
Irreführers-Verderbers, O 38.11a)."[8]   While the preaching
activity of corruption does clearly parallel that of the
perfect virgin in vss 5ff, his argument that corruption
imitates the saviour's work in "destroying destruction," ˀwbd
lˀbdnˀ in vs 2a is based on a misunderstanding of the Syriac
idiom. The expression means, as Harris and Mingana put it
(375), "he made utter destruction,"[9] which parallels in sense
vs 2b: "he corrupted all his works." The verse thus underlines the totally destructive and corrupting activity of the
subject.

Harris and Mingana (376-377) are probably correct in
seeing Proverbs as at least partially responsible for the
description of the speaker's activity in vss 3-4, as well as
for the report of the perfect virgin's preaching in vs 5 and
the speech itself in vss 6-13.[10] Like the feminine figure of
Wisdom in Proverbs, corruption lets his voice go forth (Prv
8.1: "Does not wisdom call, does not understanding raise her
voice?"), and he stands upon a high peak (Prv 8.2: "On the
heights beside the way. . . ." Prov. 9.3: ". . . she invites,
upon the heights of the town"). The description of the
activity of the speaker in vss 3-4 and especially of the
perfect virgin in vs 5ff also closely parallels the description of Jesus in Jn 7.37: "Jesus stood up and proclaimed,
saying, 'If anyone thirst, let him come to me and drink.'"
See also Jn 7.28, 12.44, 1.15.[11]

Verse 5

That the activity of the perfect virgin, no matter how
similar in appearance to that of corruption, is completely
different is emphasized by the first word of the verse l ,
"but, however." Like Lady Wisdom she too stood up (Prv 8.2
". . . in the paths she takes her stand"); just as Wisdom
calls, invites, cries in Prv 8.1-3, so she proclaims, cries,
speaks.

Verses 6-13

The vocabulary and structure of this address of the
perfect virgin has obviously been shaped by the language of
the Wisdom tradition,[12] and, like Wisdom texts such as Prv
1.20ff, 8.1ff; Sir 24.1ff; 51.1-30, follows the basic form of
mission preaching which E. Norden successfully isolated.[13]
The form underlies texts coming from different places and from
times quite distant from one another. It contains the following elements:[14]

1. An invitation to accept knowledge of the true God.

2. A promise of eternal life and everlasting happiness
   as a reward for this knowledge.

3. Sometimes as a complement to the promise, a threat of
   death or destruction for those who refuse to accept
   the invitation that has been extended to them.

4. The preacher demands a hearing and compliance with
   his or her commands because of his or her identity as
   the messenger of the divine, or as a divine figure.
   The speaker often reveals his or her identity in
   "I-am" statements.[15]

Verses 6-7

Using direct address, a commonly used formal element both
in Wisdom literature in general (e.g., Prov 8.4, 32) and in
the material gathered by Norden, and using plural imperatives,
the perfect virgin calls men and women to conversion: they
must "turn back," ʾtpnw (vs 6a), and they must "leave," šbwqw,
the ways of "that corruption," to whom, presumably, they have
been drawn. The root šbq has appeared twice before in Ode 33,
in vs 1a, "he expelled," šbqt, corruption, and in vs 3a, "he
let his voice go forth," šbq. The Odist's use of the same
root in its various shades of meaning may be intended to
reinforce the unity of his composition.

The negative commands of vss 6a and 7a are balanced by
the positive invitation in vs 6b, "come," and in vs 7b,
"approach." The choice is thus clearly drawn: follow the
ways of corruption or turn and approach the speaker, the

perfect virgin. The call to conversion is quite usual in the
Mission preaching type of texts, and frequently accompanies
the invitation to accept knowledge of the true God.[16] Wisdom
is often depicted as calling her listeners to leave evil or
corruption and to come to her, e.g., Prv 2.1ff, 12ff, 3.17,
4.11, 5.1ff, 8.4ff, 9.6; Sir 51.23.[17] The invitation "to
come" is also part of the speech of Jesus in Jn 7.37.[18]

Verses 8-9

   Verse 8 is a tricolon containing three promises formulated with first person singular imperfect verbs. The promise
of vs 8a may have its background in the image of Wisdom
entering into men. According to Prv 2.10, e.g., "For wisdom
will come into your heart" or see Wis 7.27: "Age after age
she enters into holy souls and makes them God's friends and
prophets."[19] While Ben Sirach could exhort, "Come to me, you
who need instruction, and lodge in my house of learning" (Sir
51.23), it is no ordinary teacher or preacher who promises to
enter into her listeners, but is probably a divine force or
power who speaks as the perfect virgin, perhaps divine Wisdom
herself.

   The promise in vs 9a to bring the listener forth from
destruction, mn 'bdn', repeats a theme that echoes throughout
the Ode. Corruption is described in vs 2a as the great agent
of destruction, and those who listen to and are drawn to the
preaching of corruption are within his destructive power.
From this destruction, however, the perfect virgin will free
them. The third promised result of listening to her will be
that she will make them wise, 'hkmkwn, in the ways of truth.
As Ulrich Wilckens comments, "Dass die Weisheit die Ihren
weise macht (Od.Sal. 33.8), ist überall Grundsatz der jüdischen Chokma."[20] The promise of deliverance from destruction
is repeated in vs 9. The bicolon repeats in parallel form the
two roots we have seen frequently before in Ode 33; "you will
not be corrupted, tthblwn," and "you will not be destroyed,
t' bdwn." The promise of release from or safety from destruction is both a mildly veiled threat as well as a promise, and
accords with elements 2 and 3 in Norden's schema. Though the

perfect virgin does not, in contrast to Norden's element 1,
preach knowledge of the true God, but rather, promises to make
her listeners wise, it is precisely through wisdom or knowledge that salvation is accomplished.[21]

Verses 10-11a

In a pair of imperatives in vs 10a the perfect virgin
exhorts her hearers to listen to her and be saved, and in vs
10b she provides a reason why they should comply with her
commands. The syntax of vs 10b, however, is not clear; "the
grace of God" can be construed either as the object of the
participle mmll', or as in apposition to the first person
singular pronoun, 'n', which seems more likely, given the
"I-am" statement in vs 11b. Such a self-identification is, as
we noted, a standard element in the missionary preaching.

The self-identification is followed by a promise in vs
11a. having revealed that she is the grace of God who speaks,
the perfect virgin assures her listeners that they will indeed
be saved, repeating in the imperfect the root prq which was
used in the imperative in vs 10a. The additional phrase, "you
will be blessed," is probably a pleonastic expression serving
to strengthen the promise of salvation. If we are correct in
our interpretation of vs 10b, then the perfect virgin and the
grace of God, whose actions were reported in vs 1, are the
same figure. Vss 10-11a contain Norden's elements 2 and 4.
Salvation and beatitude, the perfect virgin says in vs 11a,
will come "by my hand," b'ydy, a claim that indicates that the
perfect virgin is herself the one through whom salvation is
effected.[22]   As we saw earlier, the hypostatized figure of
grace appears as a divine agent in a variety of gnostic texts.
Not only does she bring salvation, but she is often responsible for bringing and increasing knowledge.

Verses 11b-12

This unit of thought begins with the second self-
identification of the perfect virgin. She is the judge of her
hearers, dynkwn, not in the sense of one who punishes or
threatens to punish those who refuse to accept her commands

(as in Norden's element 3), but rather, as judge she guaran-
tees and executes justice for them. See the striking parallel
in Jn 5.24ff where Jesus describes himself as the one who has
been given authority to execute judgement. The one who hears
his word and believes him who sent him has eternal life, has
passed from death to life. Jesus, like the perfect virgin,
then, is the revealer who as judge accomplishes life for the
hearer. Those who have put her on, hnwn dlbšwnny, can rest
assured that with her as their judge they shall not be
wronged, defrauded, deprived, l'nttlmwn, of what is theirs,
which, according to vs 12b, is "incorruption," l' hbl', in the
new age or world, b'lm' hdt'. The new age or world is probably to be understood as referring to the eschatological age
of salvation to which the present age is so often contrasted
in the New Testament, and which figures so prominently in
apocalyptic literature.[23] Johannes Behm remarks that ". . .
the new aeon, which has dawned with Christ, brings a new
creation, the creation of the new man."[24] Whether or not Ode
33 is seen as Christian, the incorruption which the perfect
virgin promises is probably to be understood as a characteristic of the saved in the new age; they are transformed, they
are made new, immortal, free of all corruption.[25]

It is difficult to know exactly what the Odist means by
"putting on" the perfect virgin, for, as Hans Dieter Betz
points out, the concept of clothing oneself, of putting on a
redeemer figure ". . . has a powerful and long tradition in
the ancient religions."[26] It is found in various mystery
religions, in gnostic literature,[27] and in a number of New
Testament texts.[28] What Betz says regarding Gal 3.27 ("For as
many of you as were baptized into Christ have put on Christ")
probably applies to the image in Ode 33.12, though without any
specific Christian allusion:

> . . . this phrase presupposes the christological-
> soteriological concept of Christ as the heavenly
> garment by which the Christian is enwrapped and
> transformed into a new being. The language is
> certainly figurative, but it goes beyond the dimen-
> sion of merely social and ethical inclusion in a
> religious community; it suggests an event of divine
> transformation.[29]

To "put on" the perfect virgin is not just to listen to her
and to accept her teachings, but, in this context, it probably
refers to being transformed into a new being, one who enjoys
immortality in the final age of salvation. It is not clear,
however, whether this transformation is linked with some sort
of ritual, for example, initiation. In any case, those who
put on the perfect virgin will be united to her, who, in vs
8a, promises that she will enter into them.

Verse 13

Just as the perfect virgin begins her speech in vs 6 with
direct address to her listeners, so also at the conclusion she
addresses them, calling them "my elect," gby. In the Old
Testament the elect are above all the community of Yahweh.[30]
The Qumran sectarians regard themselves as the elect, the
elite, the just remnant in a sinful and corrupt generation,[31]
and in apocalyptic in general, the notion of election is
narrowed and transferred to a restricted group.[32] In the New
Testament and the early Church the notion of election was used
extensively and developed in a variety of ways, but in almost
all cases it carries an eschatological connotation.[33] What is
of particular interest in Ode 33.13a is the qualification of
the elect as "my elect." It is the perfect virgin who sets
apart for eschatological salvation, who chooses, who elects.[34]

The plural imperative in vs 13a may be variously construed. Literally hlkw means "walk," but, as in the biblical
usage of the same verbal root, it probably means to "behave,"
"act," "live."[35] The phrase hlkw by "walk in me" probably has
more or less the sense we find in Col. 2.6: "As therefore you
received Christ Jesus the Lord, so walk in him, en autō
peripateite," which Moule translates as "conduct your lives as
incorporated in him."[36] Given the clothing imagery in vs 12,
the expression by, like the en autō in Col. 2.6, might imply
some sort of union between the perfect virgin and her elect.

The promises in 13b and c are formulated in the first
person imperfect and directed not to the "you" of the audience, as in vss 6-11, but, as in vs 12a, to "those who . . ."
It is not clear whether "those who . . ." is simply another

way of referring to "you," or if it represents a more generalized form intended for a broader audience, which includes more
than just those addressed by the perfect virgin in her speech.

Verse 13b echoes vs 8b, with "my ways," replacing "ways
of truth," perhaps indicating that the perfect virgin herself
is to be regarded as the "truth." The making known of her
ways continues the "walk" metaphor of vs 13a. The point of
the promise is that the perfect virgin will respond to those
who desire her, just as it is said of Wisdom in Wis 6.12-13:

> She is easily discerned by those who love her, and
> is found by those who seek her. She hastens to make
> herself known to those who desire her.[37]

It is not clear what is involved in the promise of her
name to those who desire her.[38] It may mean that she will
reveal to them her true identity, a name being connected with
the nature of its bearer, in which case it rather closely
parallels vs 13b. It is also possible that the promise of the
perfect virgin's name is a promise of her protection and help.
Finally, the promise of her name may mean that she promises
that she will not only reveal to them her true nature, but
will share it with them. Having put her on, they will have
her name.

We have suggested that the figure of grace is to be
identified with the perfect virgin whose speech is found in
vss 6-13. If we are correct, taken together, the report in
vss 1-5 and the speech in vss 6-13 provide us with the following picture of the redeemer figure "grace-perfect virgin":

1. Grace descends to destroy her enemy, corruption (vs
   1b).

2. Grace runs, as she has done before, and she expels
   corruption (vs 1a).

3. The perfect virgin is a preacher, who, like corruption, rises and calls and invites men and women to
   listen to her (vs 5).

4. She demands that her listeners leave corruption; she
   presents an appeal for conversion (vss 6-7).

5. She is able to dispense knowledge; she will make her
   hearers wise in the ways of truth (vs 8c), and will
   make known to them her own ways (vs 13b).

6. A special relationship of unity and intimacy exists between the perfect virgin and those whom she calls. They are to approach her (vs 7b), she will enter into them (vs 8a), they put her on (vs 12a), and she calls them her "elect," her "chosen" (vs 13), who are to live "in" her (vs 13a). She promises them her own name (vs 13c).

7. Thanks to her (vs 11b) they will enjoy salvation and beatitude. They will be safe from destruction (vss 8b), 9), they will be incorruptible in the new age (vs 12b).

8. She identifies herself as "the grace of God" (vs 10b), and as their "judge" (vs 11b).

Though most of the elements in the portrait of the perfect virgin/grace of God figure can be found in descriptions of personified Wisdom in Jewish apocalyptic and wisdom literature,[39] it is noteworthy that the figure in Ode 33 is never called "wisdom." The titles she does bear, perfect virgin and grace of God, however, might point to some common sources shared by both wisdom and gnostic literature.[40]

We already mentioned that "grace" serves as a title for one of the aeons in some gnostic systems, and the same is true of "virgin."[41] Bornkamm studies the epithets used for the figure he calls the "Muttergöttin" in the Acts Thom. 27 and 50, for example, "the compassionate mother," "silence," "the perfect compassion," "she who knows the mysteries of the chosen," "she who makes the ineffable manifest,"[42] and remarks:

> Her epithets . . . allows us to recognize in her the Mētēr, Charis, Sigē, Alētheia, the heavenly Sophia, without however reproducing the succession of the heavenly aeons about which Gnosis elsewhere speculates.[43]

More importantly for our purposes, he insists:

> At all events, it is clear that the goddess addressed is not the fallen Sophia of numerous gnostic systems, any more than is the virgin in light of the Wedding Hymn, who is undoubtedly identical with the "Mother". . . .[44]

He maintains that it is this same "Gnadengottheit" whom we meet in a number of gnostic texts, among which he mentions as first Ode 33.[45]

Whether or not we choose to label Ode 33 as gnostic
depends largely upon our definition of "gnostic." While the
Ode obviously lacks a number of elements which are usually
regarded as essential in any properly gnostic system[46] it does
seem that the Ode comes from a religious and cultural background which, like certain gnostic groups, knew of and revered
a female hypostatized divine figure related to Wisdom, who was
seen as a redeemer figure and who could be addressed as
"grace" and "virgin." In Acts Thom. 27 and 50 the female
divine figure is also called "the Holy Spirit," and it is not
impossible that we should see the perfect virgin-grace figure
of Ode 33 as a reference to the Holy Spirit.[47]

By introducing the speaker and her opponent in vss 1-5,
the Odist prepares his audience for the speech of the perfect
virgin which is to follow in vss 6-13. The report makes it
clear that the perfect virgin is grace, who descended and who
ran, as before, and that she, rather than destruction-bringing
corruption, is to be listened to. The perfect virgin is
apparently in competition with corruption for the attention
and loyalty of men and women. Having been deceived into
following corruption, whose true evil character eluded them,
men and women are now addressed and called to conversion by
the perfect virgin. In Jewish Wisdom literature, the wisdom
teacher speaks in the name of Lady Wisdom, and here the Odist
speaks for the perfect virgin, the redeemer figure, and
addresses an audience in her name. By giving the report of
her activity and her speech the Odist makes present once again
to his audience the message and offer of salvation presented
in the words of divine "grace-perfect virgin."

The move to more generalized language in vss 12-13 might
indicate that the Odist is addressing not his own community,
but a broader audience. Indeed, Ode 33 might represent a type
of poem or hymn whose context is precisely that of mission-
preaching. The report in vss 1-5 could represent the Odist's
claim to have information and revelation from the true divine
redeemer, and the speech contains the continued call of that
figure. As we noted, the transformation language of vss 12-13
might also suggest that some ritual, perhaps either initiation
or communion, is being alluded to.

CHAPTER VI

CONCLUSION

It is usual for the final chapter of a work to summarize the findings of the preceding chapters; it may be more fruitful in the present instance, however, to outline some of the avenues of study which are likely to aid us in resolving the problems of Introduction and of the interpretation of individual Odes.

As we pointed out in the introductory chapter, the task of formcritical classification and study of the Odes is an urgent one, and one which has received surprisingly little attention. Formcritical evaluation and grouping of the Odes, however, require as a prerequisite the type of careful exegesis of each Ode which was attempted for Odes 16, 31, 33, and 36. Even when one has studied each Ode individually, one must be circumspect in the use of one Ode to help in the interpretation of the language and structure of another. Some commentators presume, without ever demonstrating it, that all the Odes consistently represent the thought of the same author or school, or that they have been carefully redacted to produce a uniformity of language and thought.[1]

A more prudent course, at least initially, would be to take a neutral stance vis-à-vis the questions of unity of authorship, date, and underlying purpose for composition. It seems best to follow the approach used by Kuhn in his study of the Hôdāyôt:

> Jedes Lied ist zunächst unabhängig von wirklichen oder scheinbaren Parallelen in anderen Liedern für sich zu interpretieren, denn es darf nicht vorausgesetzt werden, dass die wohl über einen längeren Zeitraum hin entstandenen und sicherlich auf verschiedene Verfasser zurückgehenden Geimeindelieder immer mit ähnlicher Terminologie auch die gleichen Vorstellungen verbinden.[2]

To the extent that it is possible, the interpreter must
ascertain the structure, the purpose and meaning of motifs and
images within the context and intent of the individual Ode.
Only when the function, the background and significance of the
term, image, structure in one Ode have been carefully exam-
ined, can the findings be used legitimately to inform the
understanding of "parallel" Odes. All the while the interpreter must be attentive to the fact that similar forms and
parallel structures, terms and images can function quite
differently, can represent different purposes, even when used
by the same author or by members of the same school. The text
itself of the individual Ode must always remain the ultimate
criterion for understanding the language and structure of the
poem.

The search for religionsgeschichtliche parallels for the
imagery, language and mythical and religious schemata of the
Odes, which has made up the bulk of traditional research on
the Odes, is, of course, a normal and necessary component of
research into the Odes. Attention to comparable motifs, ideas
and religious schemata can, one hopes, eventually enable
scholars to locate in known theological and cultural situa-
tions, the genres and thematic complexes found in the Odes.

As in the case of apparent parallels from within the
Odes, so also with parallels from other texts and from the
literature of different traditions, one must exercise extreme
caution. The same motif, image, mythical or religious schema
may be used for radically different purposes in different
contexts.[3] Differences, then, in emphasis, deviations from
standard form, shifts in interpretation, the adaptation of
inherited texts, traditional myths, stories, images and ideas,
the presence of particular terminology, are what the scholar
must be especially sensitive to in his or her effort to
discern the identifying characteristics of the community
responsible for the Odes.[4]

Unfortunately, we are not yet at the point in the scholarship on the Odes of being able confidently to assign them
all to specific genres. Yet is it already possible to group a
number of the Odes, some on the basis of formal coherence,

others, though lacking such formal coherence, on the basis of
unity of motif, consistency of imagery, or theological con-
formity. In the later cases, we do not attain the clarity and
precision possible with form-critical categories, but we can
identify repeated thematic complexes and theological
interests.

The majority of the Odes in the collection are Individual
Confession Odes, that is, Odes in which the speaker in the
first person singular reports in the perfect tense about
events which have transpired in the past. In the case of Odes
11, 21, 35, 36, and 38, certain formal elements as well as a
common central theme and similar imagery distinguish these
Odes from other Individual Confession Odes. While it is usual
in Odes of Individual Confession for the speaker to narrate
the events surrounding his experience of or reception of
salvation, and typically in symbolic terms, in Odes 21.1 and
35.7 the speaker also makes mention of having performed a
gesture of prayer or worship, a formal element distinctive in
these Odes. In these Odes this report immediately precedes an
account of the Odist's ascent to heaven or paradise. In all
the Odes of the subgroup, the ascent of the speaker is
associated with or representative of the process of attaining
salvation. The same or similar imagery and language is used
in many of these Odes to describe the process of ascent and
the events that transpire once the speaker has arrived in the
heights. Finally, unlike other Individual Confession Odes,
the speaker in at least four of these Odes recounts at the
conclusion that he gave praise or worshipped the Lord. The
following outline illustrates the common formal elements,
themes and shared imagery.

1)   Gesture of prayer
     Ode 21.1   I lifted up my arms
     Ode 35.7   I spread out my hands

2)   Narration of salvation
     A)   Images of election/salvation
          Ode 11.1a   My heart was circumcised and its flower
                      appeared
               2a   For the Most High circumcised me by His
                      Holy Spirit
               3a   For His circumcising became my
                      salvation

Ode 35.1a   The sprinkling of the Lord shaded me
                 with serenity
     2b   And it became salvation to me

B)   Speaker is given something to drink
     Ode 11.6-7 And speaking waters came near my lips
                 From the fountain of the Lord
                    abundantly,

                 And so I drank and became intoxicated
                 From the living water that does not
                    die.

     Ode 35.5   And I was carried like a child by its
                    mother;
                 And He gave me milk, the dew of the
                    Lord.

C)   Experience of rest
     Ode 11.12a And from above He gave me immortal
                    rest.

     Ode 35.1   The sprinkling of the Lord shaded me
                    with serenity,
                 And a cloud of peace it set above my
                    head.
       4a   And I was at peace in the company of
                    the Lord
       6b   And I rested in His perfection

     Ode 38.4   And He went with me and caused me to
                    rest
                 And did not allow me to err.

D)   Ascent
     1)   Ascent proper
          Ode 11.16   And He took me to His paradise

          Ode 21.2b   And my helper lifted me up to His
                         compassion and His salvation.
              6   And I was lifted up in the light,
                      And I passed before Him.

          Ode 35.7a   And I stretched out my hands as my
                         soul ascended

          Ode 36.1b   And She lifted me up to heaven

          Ode 38.1a   I ascended to the Light of truth as
                         a chariot

     2)   Role of the Intermediary in the ascent
          Ode 21.2b   My Helper lifted me up

          Ode 36.1b   She lifted me up

          Ode 38.1b   Truth led me and caused me to come

3) Events during the ascent
  a) Stripping and clothing
      Ode 11.10   And I rejected the folly cast
                    upon the earth,
                    And I stripped it off and cast
                    it from me.
          11   And the Lord renewed me with His
                    garment,
                    And possessed me with His light.

      Ode 21.3   And I put off darkness and put
                    on light.

  b) Healing and refreshment
      Ode 21.4   And I myself acquired members,
                    having in them no
                    Sickness, nor affliction nor
                    suffering.

      Ode 11.14   And my eyes were enlightened,
                    And my face received the dew;
          15   And my breath was refreshed
                    By the pleasant fragrance of the
                    Lord.

  c) Reception of knowledge or instruction
      Ode 38.7   But truth was proceeding on the
                    upright way,
                    And whatever I did not
                    understand He exhibited to me.
         16   But I have been made wise so as
                    not to fall into the hands of
                    deceivers
                    And I myself rejoiced because
                    the truth had gone with me.

      Ode 11.4   From the beginning until the end
                    I received His knowledge.
         5   And I was established upon the
                    rock of truth,
                    Where He had set me.

E) Arrival
  1) Stand before the presence of God
      Ode 36.2   And caused me to stand on my feet in
                    the Lord's high place,
                    Before His perfection and His
                    glory . . .

      Ode 35.7b   And I stood upright in the presence
                    of the Most High

  2) Near to God
      Ode 21.7a   And I was near Him

      Ode 36.6b   And I became one of those who are
                    near Him
         8a   And my being brought near was in
                    peace

3) <u>Salvation</u>
Ode 21.2b   And my helper lifted me up to His
            compassion and His salvation

Ode 35.7c   And I was saved in His presence

Ode 38.17a For I was established and lived and
            was saved

4) <u>Established</u>
Ode 38.17a For I was established and lived and
            was saved

Ode 36.8b   And I was established in the Spirit
            of providence

5) <u>Entrance into light</u>
Ode 21.6   And I was lifted up in the light
            And I passed before Him

Ode 11.19b And have passed from darkness into
            light

Ode 38.1a   I ascended to the light of truth as
            a chariot

6) <u>Regeneration</u>
Ode 36.3a   She brought me forth before the
            Lord's face
        5   For according to the greatness of
            the Most High, so she made me;
            And according to His newness, He
            renewed me.

7) <u>Being planted in paradise</u>
Ode 11.18ff And I said, Blessed, O Lord, are
            they
            Who are planted in Thy land,
            And who have a place in Thy
            paradise . . .

Ode 38.17ff For I was established and lived and
            was saved,
            And my foundations were laid on
            account of the Lord's hand;
            Because He planted me . . .

3) <u>Praise and Confession</u>
Ode 11.17-24 Then I worshipped the Lord because
              of His magnificence.
              And I said, Blessed, O Lord, are
              they . . .

Ode 21.7-9   And I was near Him,
              Praising and confessing Him.

              He caused my heart to overflow, and
              it was found in my mouth;
              And it sprang forth unto my lips.

              Then upon my face increased the
              exultation of the Lord and His
              praise.

Ode 36.2c   While I was glorifying Him by the
                      composition of His Odes
       4a   I was praising among the praising
       7   And my mouth was opened like a cloud
                      of dew,
                      And my heart gushed forth, a gusher
                      of righteousness.

Ode 38.20   And the Lord alone was glorified,
                      In His planting and in His
                      cultivation.

The role that a study of groups within the Odes can play
in enriching the understanding of an individual Ode is clear
from the light that the Ascent Odes shed on the problems of
interpretation of Ode 36. As we noted in our study of Ode 36,
in that Ode and in the other Odes of Ascent, the speaker uses
a variety of images which he associates with ascent to describe his experience of eschatological salvation. He claims
to have been translated into the realm of the divine, already
to be enjoying heavenly or paradisial existence.[5] The fact
that a gesture accompanying prayer precedes the ascent in Odes
21.1 and 35.7 may argue for interpreting Ode 36.2c to mean
that the ascent takes place <u>while</u> the speaker was praising the
Most High by the composition of His odes.[6] It was stressed
that the events which take place before the Most High in Ode
36 center on the transformation which the speaker undergoes,
and that the birth by the Spirit, the reception of the name
"son of God," and the anointing should be interpreted as
referring to his transformation into a heavenly or divine
being.[7] This interpretation is supported by the imagery of
Ode 11.11: the speaker is clothed with the Lord's garment,
and the Lord possesses the speaker with His light; and by Ode
21.3: "And I put off darkness, and put on light."[8] On the
basis of these texts, it is likely that <u>nhyr'</u> in Ode 36.3c
means that the speaker has been filled with the light that is
symbolic of the divine nature.

In Odes 11.17-24, 21.7-9, 38.20 the climax of the ascent
consists in praise and confession, and so one is probably
justified in understanding Ode 36.7 as a reference also to
praise or confession; note Ode 36.7's close parallelism of
language with Ode 21.8 which clearly alludes to praise. Ode

38.17 describes the speaker's installation in the Lord's
presence in paradise with the expression ꜣštrrt , "I was
established," the same term which occurs in Ode 36.8b. Ode
36.8b's description of the speaker's approach to the presence
of the Most High bšlmꜣ, "in peace," agrees with Odes 11.12a,
35.1, 4a and 38.4 which connect peace, serenity, tranquility
and rest with the experience of ascent.[9] In none of the Odes
of Ascent does the ascent aim at the revelation of knowledge
of God's secret plans for the universe, the mysteries of the
universe, or with the vision of God, His throne, His court.
The ascent is the Odist's way of expressing, rather, the
experience he has of being saved, as is evident in Odes 21.2b,
35.7, and 38.17a where salvation and ascent are intimately
linked.

Ode 11.1ff also supports the contention that ascent is
connected with the transformation of the speaker. The Odist
in Ode 11.1-3 combines the agricultural image of pruning with
the image of circumcision of heart by the Holy Spirit.[10] As
Roger Le Déaut shows, the Odist builds above all on the
language of Dt 30.6.[11] The Most High, by His Holy Spirit,
circumcises the Odist's heart, with the effect of laying bare
the inmost being of the Odist before the presence of the Lord,
and fills him with the love of God. The interior transformation brought about by the Holy Spirit is salvation for the
Odist, and causes him to walk in the Lord's way, a way identified in vs 3 with the way of truth. Using the traditional
imagery of covenant renewal and interior restoration, the
Odist interprets his own interior transformation by God's
Spirit according to the model of the actualization or realization of the Lord's promise for the restoration and renewal of
His people in the new covenant. By the Spirit's circumcision
of his heart, he has entered into the state of the saved. Vss
4ff explain that this transformation is connected with the
speaker's reception of knowledge of the Most High. In vss 6-8
the Odist recalls that he became intoxicated from drinking the
living water that does not die, that comes from the fountain
of the Lord. The Odist insists that the intoxication is not
with ignorance, and vss 8-11 explain that rather than having

allowed himself to be caught up in ignorance, he has done just
the opposite, he has rejected vanity and folly, and has turned
towards the Most High. It is obvious that in Ode 11 we are
dealing with the language of conversion and transformation.

The following outline shows that the basic thematic
components of the Hellenistic missionary appeal which shape
the speech of the perfect virgin in Ode 33, are in the background of Ode 11's description of conversion and transformation, and also of Ode 15, an individual confession Ode spoken
by the Odist in the first person, in which he reports what the
Lord has done for him. It is important to note here that a
common thematic complex is employed in Odes which are formally
dissimilar.

A)   Reception of Wisdom/Enlightenment

1)   The Lord is compared to the sun
      Ode 11.13a   And the Lord (is) like the sun
      Ode 15.2a   Because He is my sun

2)   Enlightenment
      Ode 11.14   And he enlightened my eyes,
                    And my face received the dew.
      Ode 15.2b   And His rays roused me
            2c   And His light has dismissed all
                      darkness from my face.

            3   Eyes I have obtained through Him,
                    And have seen His holy day.

3)   Reception of truth
      Ode 11.3b-c   And I ran in the way of His peace,
                    In the way of truth.
            5   And I was established upon the rock of
                      truth,
                    Where he had set me.
      Ode 15.4   Ears I have acquired,
                    And have heard His truth.
      Ode 33.8c   And I will make you wise in the ways of
                      truth.

4)   Reception of knowledge
      Ode 11.4   From the beginning until the end
                    I received His knowledge.
      Ode 15.5   The thought of knowledge I have
                      acquired,
                    And have been delighted by it.
      Ode 33.13b   And my ways I will make known to them
                      who seek me

5)   Gift is for those who "seek"
      Ode 15.1   As the sun is the joy to them who seek
                      its dawning,

<pre>
                       So is my joy the Lord.
     Ode 33.13b   And my ways I will make known to them
                           who seek me
</pre>

B) Conversion

    1)   Turn from, leave
<pre>
        Ode 11.8b   But I left vanity
            10a   And I left folly
        Ode 15.6a   I left the way of error
        Ode 33.7a   Leave the ways of this corruption!
            6a   Sons of men, turn!
</pre>

    2)   Stripping image
<pre>
        Ode 11.10b   And I stripped it (folly) off and cast
                           it from me.
        Ode 15.8b   And I stripped off corruption by His
                           grace
</pre>

    3)   Turn towards, come
<pre>
        Ode 11.9a   And I turned towards the Most High, my
                           God
        Ode 15.6b   And I went towards Him and received
                           salvation from Him
        Ode 33.6b   And their daughters, come!
            7b   And approach me!
</pre>

C) Results/Benefits

    1)   Salvation
<pre>
        Ode 15.6b   . . . and received salvation from Him
                           richly
        Ode 33.10a   Listen to me and be saved!
            11a   And by my hand you will be saved
</pre>

    2)   Blessed
<pre>
        Ode 11.18   Blessed, O Lord, are they, I said,
                        Who are planted in Thy land . . .
        Ode 33.11a   . . . and you will become blessed
</pre>

    3)   Clothing imagery
<pre>
        Ode 11.11a   And the Lord renewed me with His
                           garment
        Ode 15.8a   I put on incorruption through His name
        Ode 33.12   And those who have put me on will not
                           be deprived,
                        But will possess in the new age
                           incorruption.
</pre>

    4)   Enjoyment of incorruption/eternal life.
<pre>
        Ode 11   Expressed in the image of the Odist's
                           being taken into paradise.
            11.12a   And He gave me from above rest that is
                           without corruption
        Ode 15.8a   I put on incorruption through His name,
                        And took off corruption by His grace.
            9   Death has been destroyed before my
                           face,
                        And Sheol has been vanquished by my
                           word,
</pre>

10   And <u>eternal life</u> has arisen . . . in
        the Lord's land,
        And it has become known to His faithful
        ones,
        And has been given without limit to all
        who trust in Him.

Ode 33.8b   I will bring you forth <u>from destruction</u>
       9   You will <u>not be corrupted,</u>
             <u>Nor will you be destroyed.</u>
      12b   But will possess in the new age
             <u>incorruption</u>

In Ode 11, then, the Odist combines the Old Testament image of covenant renewal and interior transformation with the language of the Hellenistic mission speech. He receives knowledge, he rejects folly, he turns to the Most High, and he is given immortal life, incorruptibility, eschatological salvation, here represented as transport into paradise.

This analysis of Ode 11 is supported by a study of its parallels with Ode 35, another Ascent Ode. As in Ode 11 the Spirit plays a major role, and preceding the ascent the Odist receives knowledge or revelation, experiences rest and is made one of the Lord's company. Ode 35 opens with an Old Testament image, as does Ode 11, the image of the overshadowing cloud.[12] Used extensively in Old Testament descriptions of the Exodus, Israel's desert wanderings, and the new Exodus, the cloud represents God's guidance and His protective presence with His people. In the Wisdom tradition Wisdom herself becomes identified with the cloud, and is seen as the guide and protector of God's people during the Exodus and throughout history.[13] In Is 63.13ff the Holy Spirit is given the functions of the cloud, that of guiding and being a protective covering; and in a number of passages from the New Testament and early Christian texts, the Spirit has assumed the functions and imagery connected with the cloud.[14]

J. Luzzaraga sees references to the Exodus tradition in nearly every line of Ode 35.[15] Vs 1, he maintains, is inspired by Num 10.34: "And the cloud of the Lord was over them by day. . . ." Vs 2 reminds Luzarraga of Ex 14.4, 15.2 and Ps 119.14 where God is described as guarding His people by means of His cloud, as with a wall, and shows Himself to be Israel's salvation. In his view, the fear and smoke and judgement of vs 3 are allusions to the destruction which terrified the Egyptians at the Red Sea, and vs 4 refers to the Israelites being led and protected under the cover of the clouds of glory. Luzarraga is less successful when he interprets the milk in vs 5 as an allusion to the white manna given to the Israelites for their nourishment, claiming that it is comparable to dew since both fall from the skies (Ex 16.14). He thinks that the dew also alludes to the springs of water opened for the Israelites in the desert.

Luzarraga is probably correct in seeing in Ode 35 close ties with the Exodus account's notion of God's protective presence and the exegetical traditions which grew up around it in the literature of Israel. The Odist, it would seem, compares his present experience of salvation with that of the Israelites in the Exodus, and perhaps also intends an allusion to the longed-for new Exodus. Luzarraga, however, fails to give sufficient attention to the curious statement that the Lord gives the Odist milk. While milk in the Old Testament serves as a symbol for blessings and abundance in general, above all it represents nourishment that sustains life, and so it is easy to understand how milk could come to represent anything which was seen to impart sustaining and life-giving nourishment to a person.[16] Texts such as 1QH 7.20-22; 1 Cor 3.1ff; 1 Pet 2.2-3; Heb 5.13ff; Clem.Alex. Paed I.35.3, 36.1, 43.3, 46.1 indicate that "milk" was used to symbolize teaching, instruction, knowledge, which is probably the sense it has in Ode 35.[17] It is also possible that milk, the food of the promised land after the Exodus, serves in Ode 35 as a metaphor for the eschatological blessings to be enjoyed in paradise.

The immediate context of the ascent in Ode 11 was the Odist's experience of conversion, his reception of knowledge, and his interior transformation brought about through the Spirit. In Ode 35 it is, as was noted, once again the Spirit, who, in the imagery of the Exodus cloud, effects salvation for the Odist, giving him rest, making him one of the Lord's company, providing him with milk, that is, instruction or revelation. The language of transformation and conversion can also be found in Ode 21.3-4, another Ascent Ode. In Ode 38, an Ascent Ode, Truth is personified and instructs the Odist throughout his ascent. He causes the Odist to rest and keeps him from error. He makes the Odist wise, "so as not to fall into the hands of the deceivers" (16a). It is likely that the "Truth" in Ode 38 also refers to the Spirit.[18]

If one is justified in reading Ode 36 against the background of the other Odes of the Ascent group, then it might be argued that in Ode 36, as in other Odes of the group, the Spirit, who is the agent of the Odist's ascent, transforms, effects the Odist's salvation by bringing him knowledge or instruction. On the basis of data from the other Ascent Odes, perhaps one can presume that interior transformation by the Spirit and conversion to the Lord has preceded the ascent. It is such action by the Spirit that is probably alluded to in the opening line of the Ode: "The Spirit of the Lord rested upon me."

Whether or not the ascent or transferral into paradise, the transformation into a heavenly being, is realized in and through a ritual is, unfortunately, not clear from the Ascent Odes. The mention, however, of the Odist lifting up his arms (Ode 21.1) and spreading out his hands (Ode 35.7), as well as the report that he was praising the Lord by composing His odes, could be taken as indications that the context if not the cause of the ascent is some sort of ritual or prayer. The conversion language and the allusions to transformation, the Exodus cloud and the circumcision of heart imagery all argue for some sort of initiation context, though the evidence remains inconclusive. Some scholars see in the drinking of water in Ode 11.7 and the reception of milk in Ode 35.5 references to baptism,[19] but, as has been shown, the images can be readily explained as representing revelation, knowledge or instruction. Whether, in addition, they also allude to sacramental celebrations, for example, initiation or communion, cannot be established.

It is not possible within the confines of this work to discuss in detail all the possible groupings of Odes. In the

remaining pages of this chapter we will describe in general
terms three groups of Odes and then will simply indicate what
other groupings might be able to be established with further
research.

Odes 12, 16, 18, and 19 form another subgroup within the
Gattung "Individual Confession Odes" which could be designated
"Theological Reflection Odes." What distinguishes these Odes
formally from other Individual Confession Odes is the presence
of a section containing theological reflection which consti-
tutes the main body of each of these Odes. In the reflection
the "I" of the speaker disappears, and no audience is addressed or referred to. The reflection sections consist of Odes
12.5-12, 16.8-19, 18.11-15, 19.2-11. The opening sections of
these Odes are not formally distinguishable from those of
other Individual Confession Odes, but they are distinctive in
their similarity of content.

In both Ode 12.5 and Ode 16.8 the beginning of the
reflection is signaled by the particle gyr. The reflection
sections of these Odes mirror the language and concerns of
Wisdom literature. In Ode 12.5-11 the reflection concerns the
Most High and His word, ptgm³, its characteristics, its role
in bringing speech, establishing concord, and bringing knowledge of God as the Creator. Through the word people come to
know the Lord. According to Ode 16.14-19 it is by means of
the word of the Lord, mlt³, that the worlds are brought into
being. Ode 18.11-15 contrasts ignorance and truth, the vain
and those who know. Ode 19.2 introduces the dramatis per-
sonae, and the main subject of the Ode, "the milk of the
Lord," which, as in Ode 35, is probably to be understood as
the wisdom or the instruction that comes from and reveals the
Father. The Odist narrates how the Spirit milks the Father's
two breasts, gives the milk-mixture to the world (or worlds)
and finally how she gives it to the virgin who becomes a
mother. Ode 12 concludes with a macarism, and Odes 16 and 18
ends with a doxology, which could be interpreted as either the
community's response to the teaching or as the speaker's own
concluding expression of praise.

In the opening verses of Ode 12 and in Ode 19.1 the Odist reports how he has received inspiration or revelation. In Ode 19 he drank the cup of milk that was brought to him; in Ode 12.1 he was filled with words of truth, and in Ode 12.3 the Lord increased in him His knowledge. Ode 18.1-3 describes the Odist's experience of transformation which included both the lifting up and enriching of his heart, and the strengthening of his limbs, the healing of his body. In the petitions in Ode 18.4-5 he prays to retain what he has received, presumably connected with the experience he has described in vss 1-3: the Lord's word, ptgm², and His perfection, šwmly² (see also Ode 19.5). It would seem, then, that in Ode 18 there is an allusion to the Odist's reception of the word. In the hymnic section of Ode 18, in vss 8-10, one finds language reminiscent of Ode 12.2-3; God's mouth is referred to, in which there is no falsehood nor death (see Ode 12.2-3). Ode 16 makes no such explicit claim to the reception of a divine word or revelation, but does insist that the reflection that follows is inspired.

The second motif of the report sections is the claim to speak or to sing by God's power or through His inspiration. In Ode 12.1 the Lord filled the Odist with words of truth, so that he might speak, and in vs 2 the Odist proclaims,

> And like a flow of waters truth has flowed from my mouth,
> and my lips have declared its fruits.

Ode 16.2 uses similar language, stressing, however, the role of the love of the Lord:

> My craft and my labour are in His praises
> Because His love provided for my heart,
> And up to my lips it gushed forth fruits.

The Odist announces that he will sing to the Lord in Ode 16.3, and in vs 5 claims that the Lord's spirit will inspire his praise:

> I will open my mouth,
> And His spirit will speak in me
> The glory of the Lord and His beauty.

In Ode 18.15 "those who knew"

> . . . spoke the truth,
> From the breath which the Most High breathed into them.

As in Ode 16.2, so also in Ode 18.1 it is the love of the

Lord which moves the Odist's heart:

> My heart was lifted up in the love of the Most High and
>   was made to abound,
> That I might praise Him by my name.

In Ode 19 the Odist makes no reference to speaking or singing,
or in any way to communicating the revelation or message he
has received. The Ode's climax, however, does consist in the
affirmation that in bearing, the virgin "made (him) manifest,
hwyt, with 'magnificence'" (vs 11c).

     It is difficult to establish the setting for such Odes,
though community worship or perhaps study in which reflection
would be presented would seem to be good possibilities.
Lacking any note of invitation, containing no promises or
incentives (and likewise, no threats) to encourage acceptance
of the message, except perhaps the macarism in Ode 12.13, it
would seem that the reflection is either originally the
private reflection of the Odist, or is intended for those who
already belong to the Odist's community, rather than for
outsiders whom he wishes to invite to accept the message and
join the community. Though some scholars have tried to
connect Ode 19 with baptism or to the Eucharist because of its
"cup of milk" imagery, such efforts remain unconvincing, and
we are left with a group of Odes lacking motifs or imagery
which would help us situate them within any specific liturgical setting. The strong influence of Wisdom language in
these Odes suggests at least that the tradition of Wisdom
played an important role in the thought world of the
community.

     The similarities in motif and imagery within the opening
reports and in the content and language of the theological
reflections is demonstrated in the following outline.

1)   <u>Opening Report</u>

    A)   Reception of revelation
        Ode 19.1   The cup of milk was offered to me,
                      And I drank it with the sweetness of
                      the Lord's kindness.
        Ode 12.1a   He filled me with words of truth
        Ode 12.3a   He increased in me His knowledge
        (Perhaps also alluded to in the petition in
        Ode 18.4   Lord, do not, because of those who are
                      wanting, cast from me your word.)

    B)   Claim to act under inspiration
        Ode 12.1   He filled me with words of truth,
                      So that I might speak it.
            2   And like a flow of waters truth has
                      flowed from my mouth,
                      And my lips have declared its fruits.
        Ode 16.5   I will open my mouth
                      And His spirit will speak in me.

    C)   Role of the love of the Lord
        Ode 18.1   My heart was lifted up in the love of
                      the Most High and was made to
                      abound,
                      That I might praise Him by my name.
        Ode 16.2   My craft and my labour are in His
                      praises,
                      Because His love provides for my heart,
                      And up to my lips it gushed forth
                      fruits.

    D)   "Fruits" and 'water" images
        Ode 16.2   See above
        Ode 12.2   And like a flow of waters truth flowed
                      from my mouth,
                      And my lips have declared its fruits.

2)   Reflection

    A)   Word
        Ode 12.5   And the subtlety of the word, <u>ptgm'</u>, is
                      without narration,
                      And like its narration so also its
                      swiftness and its sharpness,
                      And without limit its course.
            6   And at no time does it fall, but it
                      stands and stands,
                      And one cannot know its descent or its
                      way.
           10   And they were urged on by the word,
                      <u>ptgm'</u>,
                      And they knew Him who made them,
                      Because they were in concord.
        Ode 12.12   For the tent of the word, <u>ptgm'</u>, is
                      man,
                      And its truth is love.

Ode 16.7   The abundance of His tenderness,
           The power of His word, mlt'.
     8   For the word, mlt', of the Lord
              searches that which is not seen,
           And His thought that which is revealed.
    14   And the hosts are subject to His word,
              mlt'.
    19   And the worlds come into being by His
              word, mlt', and by the thought of
              His heart.

3) Conclusion

Macarism: Ode 12.13   Happy are they who by it have
                           perceived all,
                        And have known the Lord by His
                           truth.

Doxology: Ode 16.20   Glory and honour to His name.
            Ode 18.16   Praise and great beauty to His
                           name.

Odes 3, 7 and 15 form another subgroup within the Gattung
Individual Confession Odes which can be designated "Generalized Confession Odes." Like other Odes of the Gattung, these
Odes begin with a confession or report in the first person
singular of what has occurred in the past, and the consequences of those events. What is characteristic of Odes 3, 7
and 15 is a marked shift from the personal confession to an
enunciation of a general principle which extends or applies
the experience of the Odist to a larger group. Certain motifs
and images are also characteristic of these Odes.

In Ode 3.2-7, after a report that is deeply personal in
tone, the Odist formulates in vss 8-9 a generalization based
on his own experience. In vss 2-7 he reports that he has
learned to love the Lord by being loved by the Lord; he has
been united with the Beloved and is confident that because he
loves "the Son," he shall be a son. The introduction of a new
formal element is signaled in vss 8-9 by the shift in subjects: the subject of these verses is hw d, "he who." Verses
8-9 are formulated, then, as general principles in which the
Odist extends or applies his experience of transformation
through loving union to others. He who cleaves to Him who
does not die, he who chooses Life, will be immortal, living.

In other words, whoever unites himself with the Son is transformed and shares in the Son's immortality, he becomes as the
Son is.

In Ode 3.10 the Odist inserts a claim to have spoken by
the Spirit of the Lord's inspiration and with the Spirit's
guidance; hence, what he has said is guaranteed to be true.
The Ode concludes in vs 11 with three plural imperatives which
appeal, presumably, to the Odist's audience, to be wise, to
know and to wake or to be vigilant. To be wise, to know and
to wake probably all mean to receive the personal testimony
and the general principle the Odist has articulated and to act
accordingly. If they are wise, if they know, if they are
awake, they will imitate the Odist's experience. If they
follow the principle laid out in vss 8-9 they will enjoy the
benefits promised in the same verse.

In Ode 7.1-11 the speaker reports in the first person
singular the experience he has had of the Lord. The Lord has
made Himself known and the Odist testifies that he has seen
Him. The Lord has become like a man so that the Odist might
receive Him, put Him on, learn Him and not turn from Him. "To
put Him on" connotes not only intellectual recognition or
personal acceptance of revelation, but unity and identification with, transformation.

In both Ode 7 and Ode 3 the Lord is the Odist's "Beloved." While the speaker has been the recipient or object of
the blessings described in vss 1-11, in vs 12a a formal change
takes place; the subject is now "those who are his own," in
vss 12b-13 "they," and in vss 17ff, various groups. In Ode
7.12-25 the Odist explains that the Lord has revealed Himself
for the sake of others as well, and he calls for certain
groups to come and see the Lord, as he has, to come before Him
who is present, to praise Him and to receive the knowledge of
the Lord which has come in His coming. Whereas union and
transformation are the experiences attainable by others in Ode
3, in Ode 7 it is knowledge and sight, meeting, coming into
the presence of the Lord who Himself has come. In addition,
the Odist calls upon various groups and upon all creation to

receive knowledge, and to voice praise, to "confess His power
and declare His graciousness," as the concluding imperatives
in vs 26 put it. Thus, in contrast to Ode 3, the Odist looks
for a response that has its expression not only in attachment
to or acceptance of the Lord, but perhaps also in group
acknowledgement and celebration. In both Odes the Odist
experiences the Lord, seeing Him in Ode 7, loving Him and
being loved in Ode 3, and in both Odes he is united to the
Lord. In Ode 7 he asserts that others too should go out to
meet Him, know Him, for he is come, and that they should go
out and sing to Him. In Ode 3 he wants others to be united
and be transformed in the Son, as he expects to be.

Ode 15 contains a number of motifs found in Odes 7 and 3.
Once again, the Odist narrates his own personal experience.
The Lord is his joy (vs 1; see Ode 7.1-2); he has been roused
from sleep (vs 2, Ode 3.11); he has received eyes and has seen
(vs 3, Ode 7.5) His holy day; he has received ears and has
heard His truth (vs 4). He has obtained the thought of
knowledge (vs 5, Ode 7.7) and has been delighted by Him. The
Odist is, as we saw, using the language of conversion. He has
heard a message or revelation, he has received the "thought of
knowledge." As is typical in conversion language, he employs
"two-ways" imagery to report that he left the way of ignorance
and went towards the Lord, that is, presumably, on the way of
knowledge (vss 1-2, 12-13). Vss 7-8 introduce the language of
transformation: the speaker put on (see 7.4) incorruptibility, and stripped off corruption by the Lord's graciousness.
Having been so transformed, death is destroyed before him,
Sheol is rendered powerless by his word (vs 9). Verse 10
gives both theological grounding for the Odist's experience
and extends its significance beyond the Odist himself.

He has experienced what he has because "eternal life" has
arisen in the Lord's land. Vs 10b-c explain in what sense
eternal life has arisen: it has been made known, ʾtydᶜw (see
Ode 7.3) to those who believe in Him, and it has been given to
all who trust in Him. The Odist thus implies that the experience he has had of receiving the thought of knowledge, of

having been transformed is open to all who believe and trust
in Him.

The formal elements of this group and the use of similar
motifs and images are indicated in the following list.

1) Report of blessings

A) Language of love	3.3-6	7.1	
B) Theme of transform- ation	3.7	7.4	15.7-8
C) Reception of knowledge/revelation		7.7	15.5 (15.10b-c)
D) Lord is joy		7.1-2	15.1
E) Roused from sleep	(3.11)		15.2
F) Speaker saw		7.5	15.3

2) Shift in identity of recipients or subjects

Ode 3.8-9 Shift to general statement, "he who . . ."
Ode 7.12ff Shift to "those who . . ." in vs 12, to the
groups mentioned in vss 17-19, to "they" in
vss 22-23, to "any person" in vs 24, to
"His creation" in vs 25.
Ode 15.10 Shift from speaker to "those who believe in
him," and "who trust in Him."

3) Concluding imperatives

Ode 3.11 Become wise and know and wake!
7.26 Confess His power,
And declare His graciousness!

Odes 10, 17, 22, 28 and 42 are not formally similar to
one another, but they can be grouped together because in each
of them the Odist sets his own and his community's present
experiences against the background of a saviour figure's work
in the past. Moreover, in Odes 10, 17, 22 and 42 the content
of the saviour's works are quite similar. Not only do these
past events provide the Odist with a schema for understanding
the present, but he so parallels the saving work of the past
with the events in the present as to indicate that he con-
ceives the saviour's deeds in illo tempore as extending into
and as actualized in the present.

In Ode 42 the Odist recounts how in prayer he came near
to his Lord (vss 1-2), and in a speech in vss 3-10 he represents a saviour figure as present with and speaking through
his community. The community is made up of those who love the
saviour and who therefore truly grasp him (vss 3-6). There is
an indication that the community is presently experiencing
persecution (vs 7). The Odist describes the figure's love for

his community, "those who believe" in him, in terms of the
love of the groom for his bride. All this the Odist and his
community enjoy in the present. Vs 11 seems to depict the
events of a saviour's Descensus ad Inferos, and does so in
such a way as to parallel the situation and blessings of
salvation the Odist's community experiences.

In Ode 17 the Odist sets his own individual experience
against the background of the Descensus, but, in addition, he
introduces and adapts elements of the Ascent motif. He was
crowned in God, justified and saved (vss 1-2, 4); he was
liberated from vanities (vs 3-4), and transformed, so that he
seemed like a stranger (vss 4, 6). His guide was True Thought
(vs 5) and he was glorified, his understanding was raised to
the height of truth and from there the Most High gave him "the
way of His steps" (vss 7-9a). The Descensus ad Inferos
account picks up the notes of liberation, salvation, transformation and the granting of knowledge.

Ode 10 opens with the Odist's claim to possess divine
inspiration and guidance (vss 1-3). Immortal life dwells in
him, thereby empowering him to carry out a mission of preaching or teaching parallel to the mission of the saviour figure.
Though the Odist's mission is not identical with the work of
the saviour in the underworld, it is similar to it in a number
of important ways.

The Odist describes his own intimate relationship with
the Lord in Ode 28.1-8. He enjoys the protective power and,
presumably, the inspiring presence of the Spirit (vs 1). He
experiences joy and rest (vss 2-3). The Odist describes
himself as one who "believes" (vs 3; 42.9, 22.7), and employs
the rich language of human love to characterize his relationship with the Lord (vss 6-7). The Odist is confident that he
shall never be separated from his Lord, either by sword or by
blade (vs 5). Both vs 5 and vs 6, "I was prepared before
destruction should occur," suggest that the Odist faces
danger, perhaps persecution (see 42.7). He claims to possess
in himself the Spirit which is from Immortal Life (see Ode
10.2). The Odist's claim to the presence of the Spirit may
function here as a preparatory claim to divine inspiration for

what is to follow (see Ode 10.1-3). The speech in vss 9-20 recalls the persecution of a saviour figure and, parallel to vss 1-8, presents salvation and vindication as guaranteed by the special transcendent identity of the speaker and his relationship to God.

In Ode 22, unlike the other Odes of this group, the Odist's speech follows that of the Saviour. As in Ode 42.3-9, though different in form, the Odist is concerned with what God (or His "Right Hand") has accomplished for the community, "for those who believe in You" (vs 7; 42.9, 28.3). For their sakes evil's poison was destroyed and a way was leveled (vs 7; 17.4-5, 7); they were gathered from the tombs and made alive again (vss 8-10, 28.5-8, 10.2, 17.1-2[?]). The world is brought to destruction so that it might be made new (vs 11, 17.4) and the Lord has established His kingdom, the dwelling place of the saints, upon His "rock" (vs 12). In what is probably the speech of the Saviour (vss 1-6) the speaker describes how God through him, especially through his work in Sheol, accomplished the salvation the Odist's community enjoys. The account stresses the gathering of "those in the middle" (vs 2; compare vs 8), the liberation of those in bondage (vs 4; if "bondage" is bondage to death, compare vss 8-10), and the destruction of the dragon (vs 5; compare vs 7).

The parallels in motif and imagery in the saviour speeches in Odes 10, 17, 22 and 42 are quite extensive, as the chart below indicates. In all of these Odes the saviour's work seems to be set in the context of the Descensus ad Inferos motif.[20]

1.	Saviour descended		22.1	42.12
2.	Opened closed doors	17.9,11		
	smashed bars	17.10		42.17
	set them free	17.12	22.4	42.16,20
3.	Went to His own	17.12		
4.	Gave knowledge	17.13		? 42.14
5.	Sowed fruits into hearts	17.14	10.6	
6.	Changed them	17.14	(See #10)	

7.	They became alive	17.15	10.6	22.8-10	42.14
8.	Gathered them to me	17.15	10.5	22.2	42.14
9.	They are saved	17.15	10.4		42.18
10.	They become "my members, I their head."	17.16- 17	10.6 10.4	22.2	42.20
11.	Captured world		10.4		
12.	Defeated 7- headed dragon			22.5	
13.	Set at its roots			22.4	42.12
14.	Ascent from lower region			22.1	

Odes 25, 29 and 37 can also be considered Individual
Confessions, with Odes 25 and 29 connected thematically,
though not formally to the Ascent Odes. Ode 1, with its shift
from the third to the second person in referring to the Lord
should also be considered as an Individual Confession.

Odes 8, 9, 31, and 33 are Invitation Songs, that is, Odes
in which a call or an invitation is directed to a group that
is described in subordinate clauses. In Ode 8, for example,
those addressed are "you who once were brought low" (vs 3b),
"you who were silent" (vs 4a), "you who were despised" (vs
5a); in Ode 30.2 they are "all you thirsty," in Ode 31.6 "you
who were afflicted." The content of the invitation or call
expressed in imperatives varies from Ode to Ode. The imperatives in Ode 8 are, "Open, open your hearts to the exultation
of the Lord" (vs 1a), "rise and stand fast" (vs 3a), "speak"
(vs 4a), "be lifted up" (vs 5a), "hear the word of truth,
receive the knowledge of the Most High" (vs 8), "guard my
mystery, guard my faith" (vs 10), "understand my knowledge,
love me with affection" (vs 11), "pray again and again, remain
in the love of the Lord" (vs 20). The imperatives in Ode 9
are the following: "open your ears" (vs 1a), "give me your-
self" (vs 2a), "be enriched in God the Father, accept the mind
of the Most High, be strengthened and saved in His grace"
(vs 5), "put on the crown in the true covenant of the Lord"
(vs 11). Ode 30 contains these imperatives: "draw water for

yourselves from the living fountain of the Lord" (vs 1a), "come, take a drink, rest besides the fountain of the Lord" (vs 2). In Ode 31 one finds "go forth, receive joy" (vs 6), "take possession of yourselves through grace, take for yourselves immortal life" (vs 7), and in Ode 33, "return, come" (vs 6), "abandon the ways of this corruption, approach me" (vs 7), "listen to me and be saved" (vs 10), "my elect, walk in me" (vs 13).

Motives for compliance with the demand or for response to the invitation are supplied in the forms of promises, short speeches of reassurance, general explanatory statements and in statements of general principle. The grouping is only loosely defined, since the elements appear in different parts of the Odes and are often quite distinctive. Odes 13 and 20 are difficult to categorize, but seem also to be a type of Invitation Song.

Odes 39, 34, 23.1-4 are Odes of Instruction and Exhortation. In these Odes the speaker is not identified, and plays no role whatsoever. Instruction is simply presented, and imperatives are given (Ode 39.8, 34.6, 23.4). Ode 32 is a brief instruction, similar to Ode 23.1-4, but it lacks any imperatives. Odes 23.5-22 and 24 are Didactic Story Odes, with Ode 23.5-22 using highly symbolic language. Both Odes describe the coming and career of a saviour figure, with stress on his defeat of his enemies.

FOOTNOTES

CHAPTER I

[1]For the works of Harris and Mingana and of the authors cited in the next paragraphs, please see the titles listed in the bibliography.

[2]J. H. Charlesworth, "The Odes of Solomon and the Gospel of John," CBQ, 35 (1973), 320-21.

[3]V. Corwin, St. Ignatius and Christianity in Antioch (New Haven: Yale University Press, 1960), 76-77.

[4]H. J. W. Drijvers, "Kerygma und Logos in den Oden Salomos dargestellt am Beispiel der 23 Ode," Kerygma und Logos. Festschrift für Carl Andresen (ed. A. M. Ritter; Göttingen: Vandenhoeck & Ruprecht, 1979) 153-172; "The 19th Ode of Solomon. Its Interpretation and Place in Syrian Christianity," JTS 31 (1980) 337-355.

[5]H. J. W. Drijvers, "Die Oden Salomos und die Polemik mit den Markioniten im Syrischen Christentum," Symposium Syriacum 1976 (Orientalia Christiana Analecta 205; Rome: Oriental Institute, 1978) 39-55; "Odes of Solomon and Psalms of Mani. Christians and Manichaeans in Third-Century Syria," Studies in Gnosticism and Hellenistic Religions Presented to Gilles Quispel (ed. R. van den Broek and M. J. Vermaseren; Leiden: Brill, 1981) 117-130.

[6]B. McNiel, "Le Christ en vérité est Un," Irénikon 51 (1978), 201.

[7]S. Brock, Review of The Odes of Solomon, by J. H. Charlesworth, JBL, 93 (1974), 623.

[8]J. H. Charlesworth, The Odes of Solomon (Missoula: Scholars Press, 1977).

[9]M. Lattke, Die Oden Salomos in Ihrer Bedeutung Für Neues Testament Und Gnosis, (3 Vol.; OBO 25/1-3; Göttingen: Vandenhoeck und Ruprecht, 1979, 1980).

[10]J. H. Charlesworth, Papyri and Leather Manuscripts of the Odes of Solomon (Dickerson Series of Facsimiles of Manuscripts Important for Christian Origins, I; Durham: Duke, 1981).

[11]Per Beskow and Sten Hidal, Salomos Oden. Den äldsta kristna sångboken översatt och kommenterad (Stockholm: Proprius, 1980).

[12]J. Guirau and A. G. Hamman, Les Odes de Salomon (Paris: Desclée de Brouwer, 1981).

[13]H. J. W. Drijvers, "Edessa und das Jüdische Christentum," VC, 24 (1970), 292.

[14]J. Kroll, Die christliche Hymnodik bis zu Klemens von Alexandreia. Verzeichnis der Vorlesungen an der Akademie zu Braunsberg im Sommer 1921 (Königsberg, 1921).

[15]R. Abramowski, "Der Christus der Salomooden," ZNW, 35 (1936), 44-69.

[16]G. Schille, Frühchristliche Hymnen (Berlin: Evangelische Verlagsanstalt, 1965).

[17]Schille, 9.

[18]D. Robertson, "Literature, The Bible As," IDBSup (New York: Abingdon, 1976), 50.

[19]K. Beyer, "Der reichsaramäische Einschlag in der ältesten syrischen Literatur," ZDMG, 116 (1966), 242-254.

[20]H. Gunkel, Einleitung in die Psalmen, 2 ed. (Göttingen: Vandenhoeck und Ruprecht, 1966), 280.

CHAPTER II

[1]Hermann Gunkel ("Die Oden Salomos," ZNW 11 [1910] 299) insists that "Das syrische Verbum bedeutet allerdings meist zur Ruhe niederlassen, sich ausruhen." He proceeds to maintain, without any supporting evidence, that the "translator" misunderstood the text he was working with and that the Urtext would simply have read kathizesthai, and proposes the translation: "Ich liess mich nieder auf den Geist des Herrn."

[2]John Strugnell. Oral suggestion.

[3]Rudolf Bultmann (Das Evangelium des Johannes [MeyerK Abt. 2; Göttingen: Vandenhoeck & Ruprecht, 1968] 52, n.7) states categorically: "In den Od.Sal. ist das Pleroma die himmlische Welt." Franz Mussner (Christus das All und die Kirche [Trier: Paulinus, 1968] 51) is more cautious when he suggests that the word may mean either plērōma or teleiōsis in the Odes: "Welche Bedeutung jeweils an den einzelnen Stellen zutrifft, kann nur aus dem Zusammenhang erkannt werden." See also Gerhard Delling, "plērōma," TDNT 6 (1968) 298-305; R. G. Hamerton-Kelly, Pre-Existence, Wisdom and the Son of Man (SNTSMS 21: Cambridge University, 1973) 183; and Edward Lohse, Colossians and Philemon (Hermeneia; Philadlphia: Fortress, 1973) 57.

[4]In the Greeting of his letter to the Ephesians, Ignatius describes himself as tē eulogēmenē en megethei theou patros plērōmati, "blessed with greatness by the fullness of God the Father." Walter Bauer (Die Briefe des Ignatius von Antiochia und der Polykarpbrief [HNT Ergänzungs-Band; Tübingen: J. C. B. Mohr, 1920] 192) remarks, "Darunter versteht Ignatius wie sein Vorgänger die Summe alles dessen, was Gott ausmacht, eine Fülle, die sich für den religiösen Sprachgebrauch der Zeit aus Anzahl einzelner plērōmata zusammensetzt. . . ." The Odist seems to use the term in much the same way, expressing with it the fullness of the divine reality.

[5]This is the interpretation of David E. Aune (The Cultic Setting of Realized Eschatology in Early Christianity [NTS Supplements 28; Leiden: Brill, 1972] 179) who maintains that Ode 36 is one of those references to "the heavenly journey of the Odist (together with his congregation) where the object of the journey is the charismatic praise of God. . . ." He suggests that the Odist and his congregation participate in eschatological salvation ". . . through the proleptic experience of participating in the future heavenly worship of God within the setting of an earthly community assembled for worship" (183). There is no reference, however, to community participation in the experience of the speaker in Ode 36, and there is no proof that community worship is the necessary or only possible context for his composing Odes in praising the Lord, though it is a natural enough setting.

[6]Josef Kroll (Die Christliche Hymnodik, 47, n. 2) maintains that the Odes were designed to transport the singer into a state of ecstasy, as seems to have been the case in the Corp. Herm. (e.g. 13.21). In the Hekhalot literature hymns also play an important role in preparing the visionary for his mystical experience, see Ithamar Gruenwald, Apocalyptic and Merkavah Mysticism (AGJU 14; Leiden: Brill, 1980) 103-104.

[7]Charlesworth, 127. Richard Abramowski ("Der Christus der Salomooden," ZNW 35 [1935] 35) numbers Ode 36 among those Odes in which, he claims, ". . . der Mensch als filius adoptivus eine Wandlung zu Gott hin erlebt." The speaker of vss 3-8, then, is the man who has been transformed into Christ. He maintains that it is in accordance with the intention of the Odes not to differentiate clearly between Christ, the "filius proprius," and the human speaker, the "filius adoptivus": "Zwischen dem eigentlichen und dem adoptierten Sohne soll im Endergebnis kein Unterschied sein."

[8]For a study of the biblical roots of the Spirit as Mother, see Robert Murray, Symbols of Church and Kingdom (London: Cambridge University, 1975) 143-144, 312-320; for a study of the theme in early gnostic literature, A. Orbe, La Teología del Espíritu Santo: Estudios Valentinos IV (Rome: Gregorian University, 1966). The early Syrian writers were very fond of using maternal language in describing the actions and qualities of the Holy Spirit, as is pointed out by Winfrid Cramer, Der Geist Gottes und des Menschen in frühsyrischer Theologie (Münsterische Beiträge zur Theologie 46; Münster: Aschendorff, 1979).

[9]See Wilhelm Bousset, Kyrios Christos (trans. John E. Steely; Nashville: Abingdon Press, 1970) 91-98; Rudolf Bultmann, Theologie des Neuen Testaments (Tübingen: J. C. B. Mohr, 1968) 123-135; Oscar Cullmann, The Christology of the New Testament (trans. Shirley C. Guthrie and Charles A. M. Hall; Philadelphia: Westminster, 1959) 270-305; Joseph A. Fitzmyer, A Wandering Aramean. Collected Aramaic Essays (SBLMS 25; Missoula: Scholars, 1979) 102-107; Joseph A. Fitzmyer, "Nouveau Testament et Christologie: Questions Actuelles," NRT 103 (1981) 200-204; Reginald H. Fuller, The Foundations of New Testament Christology (New York: Charles Scribner's Sons, 1965) 31-33, 65, 114-115, 164-167, 232; Ferdinand Hahn, The Titles of Jesus in Christology (trans. Harold Knight and George Ogg; New York and Cleveland: The Word, 1963) 279-307; Martin Hengel, The Son of God. The Origin of Christology and the History of Jewish-Hellenistic Religion (trans. John Bowden; Philadelphia: Fortress, 1976); C. F. D. Moule, The Origin of Christology, New York: Cambridge University, 1977) 22-31.

[10]Fitzmyer, Wandering Aramean, 102-107.

[11]Hengel, The Son of God, 42. Marc Philonenko (Joseph et Aséneth. Introduction, texte critique, traduction et notes [Leiden: Brill, 1968] 86) explains the title in the following way: ". . . c'est dire qu'il est élevé à une dignité qui le place immédiatement après Dieu dans la hiérarchie céleste."

[12]Hengel, The Son of God, 42.

[13]Hengel, The Son of God, 42, n. 85.

[14]Charlesworth (128) argues that since, as he believes, the Odes have docetic overtones, the translator should guard against rendering vss 3b-c as if they were in antithetical parallelism, though this is precisely how the majority of scholars interpret the verse.

[15]Lattke (171) treats it as an adjective modifying "the son of God" ("der glänzende Sohn Gottes"); likewise Beskow and Hidal: "Guds lysande son" (49). Flemming (67), Bruston (76), Charlesworth (127), Harris and Mingana (384) understand it as a noun, "luminary," "light"; Labourt and Batiffol (33), Bernard (121), Erbetta (651) and Bauer (616) treat it as a substantive formed from the participle, some interpreting it as active, others as passive. Grammatically any one of these translations is possible.

[16]Bauer (616) contends that "Der Leuchtende ist wohl das griechische phōteinos. . . ." Gunkel's explanation is that "Phōteinos ist ein Beiwort gnostischer Äonen" ("Die Oden Salomos," 301), and Hans Conzelmann ("phōs," TDNT 9 [1974] 340) shares his opinion that the term is a gnostic one, understanding it here as part of the gnostic redeemer's self-description. Quite a different approach is taken by Bernard (121) and Tsakona (610) who regard "the illumined one"

as one who has received Christian baptism and who has consequently become a son of God.

[17]E.g. 2 Bar 49.2, 51.10ff; 1 Enoch 104.2ff, 108.12ff;
Esr 7.97, 19.1; Wis 3.7; Dan 12.3. Paul Volz (Die
Eschatologie der jüdischen Gemeinde im neutestamentlichen
Zeitalter [Tübingen: J. C. B. Mohr, 1934] 397) notes that
both the notions of transformation into an angelic being and
being filled with light are connected with transformation into
a new divine being:

> Mit dem Gedanken der Engelgleichheit berührt sich
> die Vorstellung, dass die Bürger der Heilszeit und
> die Seligen Lichtgestalten sind, und doxa erhalten,
> und in beiden kommt gleicherweise zum sichtbaren
> Ausdruck, wie die Glieder des Heils der Gestalt und
> dem Wesen nach eine Verwandlung zu neuen göttlichen
> Menschen durchmachen.

[18]Charlesworth (127) follows Harris and Mingana (384) in
interpreting mšbh followed by b as a superlative. Although
this is possible grammatically, it overlooks the obvious
intentional parallelism of the Syriac: A.B.C.D./B'.C'.D'.

[19]This term is analogous to the biblical śr, which, as J.
Strugnell points out, is the usual term for archangels and
angelic princes in later Rabbinic angelology. The term
appears in 4Q S139 ("The Angelic Liturgy at Qumran - 4Q Serek
sîrôt ʿôlat haššabbāt," Congress Volume (VTSup7; Leiden:
Brill, 1960) 324, n.1).

[20]Gunkel sugggets ". . . das göttliche Geschenk
entspricht in seiner Grösse der Grösse Gottes" (Reden und
Aufsätze [Göttingen: Vandenhoeck & Ruprecht, 1913] 186).

[21]Charlesworth (127) translates hwdtʾ as "newness."
According to Payne Smith (1208), however, the word means
"initiatio, dedicatio; renovatio, restitutio." Accordingly
Lattke (171), Bauer (616) and Flemming (67) render it as
"Erneuerung"; similarly Beskow and Hidal (49), "förnyelse."
Gunkel (Reden, 186) understands the suffix as an objective
genitive, ". . . die Erneuerung, die er erfahren hat, ist ganz
wie die Erneuerung, mit der sich Gott selber ständig erneut."
It is also possible to read it as a subjective genitive, in
which case the verse would mean that the Odist experiences a
renewal effected by the Most High Himself. Bruston's suggested emendation (76), "Et selon sa joie il n'a rejoui," is
completely unnecessary.

[22]Erbetta interprets the anointing as "l'investitura
ufficiale," whereby the ". . . rapito diviene familiare
dell'Altissimo" (652). Bauer comments that with the anointing
the Odist wins "Zugang zu ihm und damit den festen Grund des
Heils" (616).

[23]See, for example, 2 Enoch 22.

[24]The speaker's mouth being opened in vs 7a is parallel to his heart gushing forth, gs°, like a gusher, $gsyt^{\circ}$, of righteousness in vs 7b. Similar phraseology occurs in Odes 40.2 and 16.2, which suggests that what comes forth from his mouth may well be praise:

As a fountain sends forth, gs°, its water,
So my heart sends forth, gs°, the praise of the
Lord,
And my lips bring forth praise to Him. (Ode 40.2)

My art and my service are in His praises,
Because His love has nourished my heart,
And His fruits He sent forth, gs°, unto my lips.
(Ode 16.2)

[25]For "cloud of dew" see Is 18.4. Carmignac ("Un qumrânien converti au Christianisme: l'auteur des Odes de Salomon," in Qumran-Probleme [ed. H. Bardke; Berlin: Akademie-Verlag, 1963] 82) claims that 36.7 represents an example of the Odist's useof "formules qumrâniennes," specifically, one found in IQH 8.16. A closer parallel is found in 1QS 11.5-7, but neither is especially close to our text, and neither helps to illumine the meaning of the simile in our context.

[26]It is significant to note that in two other Odes which treat of ascent to God's presence in heaven the Odist also uses the term $\check{s}lm^{\circ}$ in conjunction with the experience he undergoes; see Ode 35.1b and Ode 11.3.

[27]See Gerhard von Rad, "eirēnē," TDNT 2 (1964) 402-406.

[28]The same expression $^{\circ}\check{s}trrt$, "I was established," is used in Ode 38.17, another ascent Ode, to describe the Odist's installation in the Lord's presence in heaven:

For I was established and lived and was saved.
And my foundations were set by the hand of the Lord,
Because He has planted me.

[29]See D. W. Bousset, "Die Himmelsreise der Seele," ARW 4 (1901) 136; Morton Smith, Clement of Alexandria and a Secret Gospel of Mark (Cambridge: Harvard University, 1973) 238; Hans Bietenhard, Die himmlische Welt im Urchristentum und Spätjudentum (WUNT 2; Tübingen: J. C. B. Mohr, 1951) 161-191; D. W. Bousset, Die Religion des Judentums im späthellenistischen Zeitalter (HNT 21; Tübingen: J. C. B. Mohr, 1926) 275ff.

[30]See Smith, Secret Gospel, 241. Smith posits, "This orientation might derive from its founder."

[31]Hans Jonas (The Gnostic Religion [Boston: Beacon Press, 1963] 165) remarks:

The celestial journey of the returning soul is

indeed one of the most constant common features in
otherwise widely divergent systems, and its significance for the gnostic mind is enhanced by the fact
that it represents a belief not only essential in
gnostic theory and expectation, and expressive of
the conception of man's relation to the world, but
of immediate practical importance to the gnostic
believer, since the meaning of gnosis is to prepare
for the final event, and all its ethical, ritual,
and technical instruction is meant to secure its
successful completion.

[32]See Rudolf Bultmann's classic description of the
redeemer myth in Primitive Christianity (trans. R. H. Fuller;
Cleveland and New York: Meridian Books, 1956) 163-64; and in
his Theology of the New Testament (trans. Kendrick Grobel; New
York: Charles Scribner's Sons, 1951) 1.164-183. Walter
Schmithals also reconstructs the myth of the descent and
ascent of the gnostic redeemer in Die Gnosis in Korinth
(FRLANT 66; Göttingen: Vandenhoeck & Ruprecht, 1956) 82-134.
Carsten Colpe (Die religionsgeschichtliche Schule:
Darstellung und Kritik ihrer Bilder vom gnostischen Erlöser-
mythus [FRLANT 78; Göttingen: Vandenhoeck & Ruprecht, 1961]
claims that Bultmann's "typical" gnostic redeemer myth is an
abstraction, obscuring the variety of actual gnostic myths in
the extant texts. See also Colpe, "Der erlöste Erlöser," Der
Islam 32 (1957) 195-214, and "New Testament and Gnostic
Christology," Religions in Antiquity. Essays in Memory of E.
R. Goodenough (ed. Jacob Neusner; Leiden: Brill, 1968)
230-237. For a response to Colpe's criticisms see J. M.
Robinson's review of Die religionsgeschichtliche Schule in JBL
81 (1962) 287-289. Leander E. Keck (A Future for the Historical Jesus [Philadelphia: Fortress, 1980] 144-145) offers the
following balanced judgement on the present state of the
discussion:

> The reconstructed myth, and especially the means by
> which it was recovered, have been criticized repeat-
> edly, though little that is more convincing has been
> proposed in its stead. One must not confuse neces-
> sary refinements and movements toward precision with
> repudiation wholesale.

The question is discussed in light of the Nag Hammadi texts in
Craig A. Evans, "Current Issues in Coptic Gnosticism for New
Testament Study," Studia Biblica et Theologica 9 (1979)
109-113, and in George W. MacRae, "Nag Hammadi and the New
Testament," Gnosis, Festschrift for Hans Jonas (ed. Barbara
Aland; Göttingen: Vandenhoeck & Ruprecht, 1978) 148-150.

[33]See the careful judgements of Arthur Darby Nock in
Early Gentile Christianity and its Hellenistic Background (New
York: Harper, 1964) XIV. Keck (A Future for the Historical
Jesus, 147) stresses that Gnosis did not invent the myth but
employed older ideas and myths which it shaped into a new
world view. He suggests:

It may well be the case that one impact of Christianity on the Hellenistic world was to precipitate
a clear myth of the descending/ascending savior out
of the somewhat diffuse mythic ideas and patterns
already extant in the culture. (112-113)

[34]See also the outline and discussion proposed by Edwin
Yamauchi, Pre-Christian Gnosticism (Grand Rapids: Eerdmans,
1973) 29-30.

[35]See, however, Ode 22. 1-2:

He who caused me to descend from on high,
And to ascend from the regions below;

And He who gathers what is in the middle,
And throws them to me. . . .

[36]For a discussion of the myth, the problem of its
origins, and its relationship to the gnostic Sophia myth see
George W. MacRae, "The Jewish Background of the Gnostic Sophia
Myth," NovT 12 (1970) 86-101. See also Max Küchler, Frühjüd-
ische Weisheitstraditionen. Zum Fortgang weisheitlichen
Denkens im Bereich des frühjüdischen Jahweglaubens (OBO 26;
Freiburg: Universitätsverlag, 1979) 15-62; B. L. Mack, Logos
und Sophia: Untersuchungen zur Weisheitstheologie im hellen-
istischen Judentum (Göttingen: Vandenhoeck & Ruprecht, 1973);
Ulrich Wilkens, "sophia," TDNT 7 (1971) 507-509.

[37]For example, Sir 24; Bar 3.27-4.4; Wis 6-10; 2 Esdras
5.9-10; 2 Bar 48.36; 1 Enoch 41. 1-2; Prov 1.20-23; Job
28.12-28.

[38]MacRae ("The Jewish Background," 92) explains that this
is because "Jewish Wisdom writers wished to claim that Wisdom
finds a home in Israel, sometimes by the (undoubtedly secondary) identification of Wisdom and the Law."

[39]See Charles H. Talbert, "The Myth of a Descending-
Ascending Redeemer in Mediterranean Antiquity," NTS 22 (1976)
418-420; Frances Young, "Two Roots or a Tangled Mass," in The
Myth of God Incarnate (ed. John Hick; Philadelphia:
Westminster, 1977) 88-93.

[40]See, for example, the old story of the visit of Jupiter
and Mercury to Baucis and Philemon as retold by Ovid, Metamor-
phoses 8.626.721. See also Celsus' comments on the idea of
God coming down to earth in Origen, Contra Celsum 4.2.3ff, and
his description of the many prophets who wandered throughout
Palestine saying, "'I am God, or a son of God, or a divine
Spirit'" (8.9). See the story in Acts 14.11ff where Paul and
Barnabas are taken for appearances of Hermes and Jupiter.

[41]Hans Dieter Betz, Lukian von Samosata und das Neue
Testament (TU 76; Berlin: Akademie-Verlag, 1961); G. Petzke,

Die Tradition von Apollonius von Tyana und das Neue Testament
(Leiden: Brill, 1970).

[42]Talbert, "The Myth of a Descending-Ascending Redeemer,"
422-430.

[43]Young, "Two Roots," 111-112.

[44]Jonas, The Gnostic Religion, 165.

[45]See the study of J. D. Turner, "The Gnostic Threefold
Path to Enlightenment," NT 22 (1980). He notes:

> The three-state ascent of Allog, Zost and 3StSeth
> seems to have as its object not so much a vision of
> the upper world, but rather the actual assimilation
> of the state of one's own soul to the state of being
> that characterizes each level; one undergoes the
> ascent according to a prescribed sequence of mental
> states characterized by increasing self-unification
> and mental abstraction. . . Because the monistic
> ontology is emanationistic, evolving from one to
> many, the ascent is a gradual purification and
> reintegration of the timebound self, alienated from
> its ground, back to its atemporal self-identity.
> (343)

[46]Carsten Colpe, in his excellent study of the ascent
motif ("Die Himmelsreise der Seele," Le Origini dello Gnos-
tismo. Colloquium di Messina, 13-18 Aprile 1966; Testi e
Discussioni [ed. Ugo Bianchi; Supplements to Numen 12; Leiden:
Brill, 1967] 439), stresses that ". . . das Mythologem von der
HdS nicht schon als solches gnostisch ist, sondern erst da, wo
es in die salvator-salvandus Konzeption eingefügt ist." In
Ode 36 we do not have a case of an upper macrocosmic soul
serving as redeemer of a lower microcosmic soul by rousing the
lower soul from the sleep of the flesh.

[47]Bousset, Kyrios Christos, 270.

[48]Bousset, Kyrios Christos, 270.

[49]Bousset, Kyrios Christos, 270.

[50]Helmut Koester, Introduction to the New Testament
(Philadelphia: Fortress, 1982) 2.217.

[51]Koester, Introduction, 2.217. Koester parts company
with Bousset, however, in the matter of identifying this Ode
and the collection as a whole as "gnostic":

> It is still an open question whether the Odes of
> Solomon should therefore be called a gnostic hymn-
> book. Although the gnostic character of many of
> these concepts cannot be doubted, it is quite likely
> that gnostic images and terms expressing the

individual's hope for a future life and resurrection
were not limited to communities committed to gnostic
theology but had become much more widespread. If
this is the case, this oldest Christian hymnal
attests that Gnosticism affected the language of
early Christian piety in Syria very deeply indeed.
(218).

See also D. A. Aune (Cultic Setting, 26) who argues that the
common religio-historical background of the Odes is a "gnos-
ticizing tendency within Jewish Christianity." See also the
resume of literature in James H. Charlesworth, "The Odes of
Solomon - Not Gnostic," CBQ 31 (1969) 357-369, and the studies
of Kurt Rudolph, "War der Verfasser der Oden Salomos ein
"Qumran-Christ"? Ein Beitrag zur Diskussion um die Anfänge
der Gnosis," RevQ 4 (1964) 523-555; "Perlenlied und Oden
Salomos," ThR 34 (1969) 214-224; Die Gnosis: Wesen und
Geschichte einer Spätantiken Religion (Göttingen: Vandenhoeck
& Ruprecht, 1978) 34, 73, 140, 236.

[52]For apocalyptic see Bousset, "Die Himmelsreise der
Seele," 138-143, and the comparable material in Greek and
Latin literature mentioned by Smith, Clement of Alexandria,
238-240 and Jacques Schwartz, "Le voyage au ciel dans la
littérature apocalyptique," in L'Apocalyptique (Etudes
D'Histoire Des Religions 3; ed. M. Philonenko and M. Simon;
Paris: Librairie Orientaliste Paul Geuthner, (no date)
91-126. For the Merkavah material see Ithamar Gruenwald,
Apocalyptic and Merkavah Mysticism; "The Jewish Esoteric
Literature in the Time of the Mishnah and Talmud," Immanuel 4
(1974) 37-46; H. Odeberg, "Foreställningarna om Metatron i
äldre judisk mystik," Kyrkohistorisk Årsskrift 27 (1927) 1-20;
Gershom Scholem, Jewish Gnosticism, Merkavah Mysticism and
Talmudic Tradition (New York: Jewish Theological Seminary,
1960), Major Trends in Jewish Mysticism (New York: Schocken
Books, 1954) 40-79, On the Kabbalah and Its Symbolism (New
York: Schocken Books, 1965); Morton Smith, "Observations on
Hekhalot Rabbati," in Biblical and Other Studies (ed. A.
Altmann; Cambridge: Harvard University, 1963) 142-160; G.
Vajda, "Jewish Mysticism," Encyclopaedia Britannica 10 (15th
ed.; 1974) 184-185.

[53]For a discussion of the motives for pseudonymity, see
John J. Collins, The Apocalyptic Vision of the Book of Daniel
(HSM 16; Missoula: Scholars, 1977) 68-70.

[54]Susan Niditch, "The Visionary," Ideal Figures in
Ancient Judaism (SBLSCS 12; ed. G. W. E. Nickelsburg and J. J.
Collins; Missoula: Scholars, 1980) 158-159.

[55]John J. Collins "The Apocalyptic Technique: Setting
and Function in the Book of Watchers," JBL 44 [1982] 91-111)
stresses that all Jewish apocalyptic reflects some sort of
crisis. Although he regards consolation and exhortation as
typical illocutions of apocalyptic, he sees the method, rather
than the message as distinctive of apocalyptic:

> Not all apocalypses share the journey motif, but all involve a revelation of transcendent reality which is both spatial and temporal. I suggest that the typical apocalyptic technique lies in the transposition of the frame of reference from the historical crisis experienced by the author to this transcendent world. The transposition may be accomplished through mythological allegory or celestial geography or by both (as in the Book of Watchers). . . . The apocalyptic vision does not, of course, have a publicly discernible effect on the historical crisis, but it provides a resolution in the imagination by evoking a sense of awe and instilling conviction in the revealed knowledge it imparts. This technique, rather than a specific Sitz im Leben or a particular message, is what I find to be characteristic of the genre apocalypse. (111)

There is no hint in Ode 36 that the speaker is responding to a historical crisis, or that he has some revealed knowledge to offer his community as a guarantee of hope or as a means of distracting it from its plight.

[56]Küchler, _Frühjüdische Weisheitstraditionen_, 67ff.

[57]Niditch, "The Visionary," 159-160.

[58]According to I. Gruenwald (_Apocalyptic and Merkavah Mysticism_, 99), ". . . the whole of the Hekhalot literature might be defined as technical guides or manuals for mystics." Such texts provide the technical know-how for the would-be mystic:

> These technical details, the "praxis" of the mystical experience generally consist of special prayers or incantations, or prolonged fasts and special diets, of the utterance of magical names and the use of magical seals, and of ritual cleansing of the body. Although some of those means are already known from apocalyptic literature, their description in the Hekhalot literature is more detailed. They are also known from non-Jewish mysticism and magic. (99)

[59]See notes 5 and 6. See, for example, in Apoc Abraham 17 the long hymn which Abraham's angelic guide teaches him and sings with him. C. Rowland ("The Visions of God in Apocalyptic Literature," _JSJ_ 10 [1979] 152) suggests,

> Although in the Apocalypse of Abraham the recital of the hymn does not seem to be a necessary prelude to acceptance into the divine presence, it may be no coincidence that we are told that Abraham learnt to recite it _before_ he came into the presence of God.

Gruenwald (_Apocalyptic and Merkavah Mysticism_, 103) maintains that the angel taught Abraham the hymn ". . . in order to protect the visionary and to strengthen him against the things he experienced in heaven."

[60]The Ode depicts the ascent as proceeding simply from this world to the divine world. In this regard, what Gruenwald (Apocalyptic and Merkavah Mysticism, 62) notes concerning Rev 4 applies equally to Ode 36:

> There is no plurality of heavens in the book and this might mean that the book was primarily conceived either in circles which had not adapted the idea or by someone who had simply ignored what was becoming a central concept or fashion in Jewish apocalyptic.

[61]See, however, Ode 38, where the speaker describes how he passed over "chasms and gulfs," and saw "the bride and the bridegroom."

[62]Gruenwald, Apocalyptic and Merkavah Mysticism, 31.

[63]In Old Testament visions of the heavens, as well as in apocalyptic and pseudepigraphical literature, the heavens very often resound with singing, rejoicing and celestial liturgies, see, for example, Is 6.3; Rev 4.8ff, 14.2-3, 19; Enoch 39.71. The same is true of the Hekhalot literature. K.-E. Grönzinger ("Singen und Ekstatische Sprache in der frühen jüdischen Mystik," JSJ 11 [1980] 67) characterizes the heavenly throne-world as ". . . eine Welt voller Gesang und Jubel, deren Zeit in vielfältigen gesungenen Liturgien einherschreitet."

[64]See note 17 and Bousset, Die Religion des Judentums, 276: "Aber es fehlt doch nicht an Zeugnissen dafür, dass man das zukünftige Leben wirklich als ein ewiges und zugleich als ein überweltliches, auf eine neue Daseinsstufe erhobenes Leben erfassen lernte. . . .

[65]Aune, Cultic Setting, 186.

[66]Aune, Cultic Setting, 187.

[67]Aune, Cultic Setting, 194.

[68]H.-W. Kuhn, Enderwartung und gegenwärtiges Heil (Göttingen: Vandenhoeck & Ruprecht, 1966).

[69]Ode 36 is notably different, however, from the Qumran Angelic Liturgy published by J. Strugnell ("The Angelic Liturgy at Qumran," 320) who characterizes it in the following manner:

> This is no angelic liturgy, no visionary work where a seer hears the praise of the angels, but a Maskil's composition for an earthly liturgy in which the presence of the angels is in a sense invoked and

in which - an idea to which there are parallels in Christian and Jewish literature after the Epistle to the Hebrews - the Heavenly Temple is portrayed on the model of the earthly one and in some way its service is considered the pattern of what is done below.

For a discussion of Christian use of the motif of praise offered to God in the company of His angels, see Erik Peterson, Das Buch von den Engeln (München: Kösel, 1955); W. Cramer, Die Engel-Vorstellung bei Ephräm dem Syrer (Orientalia Christiana Analecta 173; Rome: Gregorian, 1965); for a discussion of human beings' participation in the angelic community see P. Schäfer, Rivalität zwischen Engeln und Menschen (Berlin: de Gruyter, 1975) 33ff.

[70]M. Delcor, "Le vocabulaire juridique, cultique et mystique de l'"initiation" dans la secte de Qumrân," Qumran-Probleme, 129.

[71]Aune, Cultic Setting, 244.

[72]Aune dismisses too hastily the fact that this Ode, like the majority of the Odes in the collection, is formulated as a narrative in the first person singular. He seems simply to assume, "In the Odes, as in the Qumran community . . . this is probably a communal rather than individual experience" (Cultic Setting, 179, n.2). For the Hôdāyôt, see Svend Holm-Nielsen, "'Ich' in den Hodajoth und die Qumrangemeinde," Qumran-Probleme, 217-229.

[73]See Bousset's discussion of the role and importance of personal prayer in Judaism of this period in Die Religion des Judentums, 176-179, 365ff.

[74]See, for example, Joseph and Aseneth, which depicts Aseneth as the model or prototypical proselyte, and describes her conversion from idolatry and her initiation into Judaism. G. W. E. Nickelsburg (Jewish Literature Between the Bible and the Mishnah [Philadelphia: Fortress, 1981] 262) maintains that "The rituals of Aseneth's conversion almost certainly betray the influence of descriptions of non-Jewish initiatory rites." Whether or not the language and rituals are precisely those which would have been used in a Jewish community cannot be established with certitude, but the rituals and language employed in the text were at least used or could be understood in the author's community to express the process of conversion and the effects of conversion. See also the discussion in J. H. Charlesworth (The Pseudepigrapha and Modern Research (SBLSCS 7; Missoula: Scholars, 1976) 137-140.

[75]Jonas (The Gnostic Religion, 166-167) argues,

The terminology of "rebirth," "reformation" (metamorphosis), "transfiguration" was coined in the context of these rituals as part of the language of the mystery cults. The meanings and applications that could be given to these metaphors were wide enough to make them fit into various theological systems, their prima-facie appeal being "religious" in general rather than dogmatically specific.

[76]See, however, Kurt Rudolf (Die Gnosis, 237) who contends that Ode 36 and other Odes describing the ascent into the heavens were sung in ceremonies in which the ascent was cultically realized:

> Die Lieder beschreiben die Gegenwart der Erlösung als bereits erfolgte "Himmelfahrt der Seele," und es scheint, dass verschiedene von ihnen, die diesem Thema gewidmet sind, bei einer "Seelenaufstiegszeremonie" oder "Totenmesse" gesungen wurden.

In a series of articles, Geo Widengren claims to find in both gnostic and Christian texts which connect ascent and baptism or initiation a schema of enthronement and coronation that can be traced back to ancient Mesopotamian times: "Den himmelska intronisationen och dopet," Religion Och Bibel (Nathan Söderblom-Sällskapets Årsbok 5; Stockholm: Svenska kyrkans Diakonistyrelses Bokförlag, 1946) 28-61; "Baptism and Entronement in Some Jewish-Christian Gnostic Documents," in The Saviour God. Comparative Studies in the Concept of Salvation Presented to Edwin Oliver James (ed. S. G. F. Brandon; Manchester: Manchester University, 1963) 205-217; "Heavenly Enthronement and Baptism. Studies in Mandaean Baptism," in Religions in Antiquity. Essays in Memory of Erwin Ramsdell Goodenough (Supplements to Numen, 14; ed. Jacob Neusner; Leiden: Brill, 1968) 551-582; "Réflexions sur le Baptême dans la Chrétienté Syriaque," in Paganisme, Judaisme, Christianisme. Mélanges offerts à Marcel Simon (ed. A. Benoit, M. Philonenko, C. Vogel; Paris: Editions E. Boccard, 1978) 347-357. It is possible that some form of enthronement ritual or motif stands behind details such as the anointing in vs 6 and the giving of the name in vs 3, but if so, it is peculiar that precisely crowning and enthronement are absent from the account of the ascent in Ode 36. In contrast see the strong and obvious impact of enthronement language in Mandaean texts (see Eric Segelberg, Masbūtā. Studies in the Ritual of the Mandaean Baptism [Uppsala: Boktryckeri Aktiebolag, 1958]) and Syrian Christian baptismal practices (Gabriele Winkler, "The Original Meaning of the Prebaptismal Anointing and its Implications," Worship 52 [1978] 24-44; "Zu frühchristlichen Tauftradition in Syrien und Armenien unter Einbezug der Taufe Jesu," Ostkirchliche Studien 27 [1978] 281-306).

[77]J. Wickham (Review of Charlesworth, JSS 20 [1975] 122) argues that a non-liturgical milieu is perfectly appropriate for the Odes, and suggests that the "I-style" of the Odes might better fit "private" poetry. See also the older literature cited in Aune, The Cultic Setting, 174-175, n. 4.

CHAPTER III

[1]Gerhard Kittel, Die Oden Salomos, einheitlich oder überarbeitet? (Beiträge zur Wissenschaft vom Alten Testament 16; Leipzig: Hinrichs' sche Buchhandlung, 1914) 22.

[2]The editorial activity would also have involved changing the masculine singular participle bs' to the feminine bsy' to agree with the feminine substantive mlt'. Theodor Nöldeke (Kurzgefasste Syrische Grammatik [Reprint of second edition; Darmstadt: Wissenschaftliche Buchgesellschaft, 1966] 58, #87) reports that mlt' is normally feminine, and masculine "nur als dogmatischer Ausdruck ho logos (künstlich)." "The Lord" would make perfectly good sense as the subject of bs'.

[3]Kittel, Die Oden, 22; Richard Abramowski, "Der Christus der Salomooden," ZNW 35 (1936) 52.

[4]Hermann Gunkel, Reden und Aufsätze (Göttingen: Vandenhoeck & Ruprecht, 1913) 190. God's activity in creation is a prominent theme in Old Testament psalms that belong to the Gattung "Hymn"; see Gunkel, Einführing in die Psalmen (Göttingen: Vandenhoeck & Ruprecht, 1933) 76-77; Hans Joachim Kraus, Psalmen (BKAT 15; Neukirchen: Neukirchener Verlag, 1960) 1. XLII. Concerning the forms used in "nature hymns," E. Gerstenberger ("Psalms," in Old Testament Form Criticism [ed. John H. Hayes; San Antonio: Trinity, 1974] 213) remarks, ". . . we have to say with Gunkel and Mowinckel that the songs in their praising parts use a variety of expressions and each composition is very far from following any set pattern or schedule."

[5]While beginning with a simile is unusual in the canonical Psalter, it is relatively frequent in the Odes, see Odes 6, 7, 14, 15, 20, 40.

[6]Harris (quoted in Harnack, 45) compares vs 1 with Stoic thought, especially that of Epictetus, e.g. Disc I. 16. Harris himself grants that "It may well have been a popular religious quotation in the latter part of the first century." As Harnack, however, remarks, precisely because the thought was so wide-spread in late antiquity, there is no convincing evidence for direct dependence on Epictetus. The similarity between Ode 16.1 and Disc I. 16, moreover, is not especially strong, and the contexts are quite different.

[7]See also in James 3 the images of the guide and helmsman or pilot. See Dibelius' discussion of the previous associations of the metaphors in A Commentary on the Epistle of James (trans. Michael A. Williams; Hermeneia; Philadelphia: Fortress, 1976) 181-195.

[8]For a discussion of the role of the speaker in the life of his community, see David E. Aune, "The Odes of Solomon and Early Christianity," given at the Society of New Testament Studies, Toronto, August, 1981, 10-11. He maintains,

Though the evidence is not clear, it appears that
the Odist represents a group of singers (perhaps
even their leader) who constitute a defined and
recognizable group within the community. (11)

Gunkel ("Die Oden Salomos," ZNW 11 [1910] 325) describes him
as:

> . . . ein gewaltigschwungvoller Dichter, ein Inspi-
> rierter und Verzückter, ein Verkündiger der Er-
> kenntnis von wunderbarem Selbstbewusstsein (7, 17),
> Vorbeter und Prediger seiner Gemeinde, zugleich
> Missionsprediger in grösstem Stil, Priester des
> Herrn, wie er sich selbst nennt (20.1) und Diener
> des göttlichen Trankes wie wir ihn mit seinen Worten
> nennen können (6, 12), jedenfalls eine überragende
> Persönlichkeit.

Abramowski ("Der Christus der Salomooden," 58) argues that the
"I" who speaks in this Ode and in all the "Individualoden" is
". . . ein hervorragendes Glied der in den Oden sichtbaren
Gemeinschaft und ihr Kultträger." The picture which these
three scholars present of the speaker is, of course, a compos-
ite based on data drawn from all the Odes of the collection.
All three authors share the widely held position that the Odes
represent "a homogenous collection of Christian hymns put into
final form by a single author-editor" (see Aune, The Cultic
Setting of Realized Eschatology [NTS Supplements 28; Leiden:
Brill, 1972] 174).

[9]See H. Ludin Jansen, Die Spätjüdische Psalmendichtung.
Ihr Entstehungskreis und ihr "Sitz im Leben" (Oslo: Jacob
Dybwad, 1937) 95-125; Svend Holm-Nielsen, "Religiöse Poesie
des Spätjudentum," Aufstieg und Niedergang der römischen Welt
19.1 (1979) 152-186.

[10]In at least Odes 8.2, 10.2, 14.7, 12.2 "fruits" seems
to refer to some sort of inspired speech or song. See Aune,
"The Odes of Solomon," 10. The image of the Lord's praises or
hymns gushing or pouring out occurs also in Ode 40.2, and
probably in 36.7. For the connection between heart and
inspired speech see 21.8-9, 26.2, 37.2-3. Tj. Baarda ("'Het
Uitbreiden Van Mijn Handen Is Zijn Teken' Enkele notities bij
de gebedshouding in de Oden van Salomo," in Loven En Geloven
Fst. H. Ridderbos [Amsterdam: Uitgeverij Ton Bolland, 1970]
249) connects the "fruits" that poured forth from the speaker's lips in Ode 16.2 and the characterization of the speaker's activity as work with the language of Ode 37.2-3:

> De vruchten van mijn moeiten waarover de dichter van
> Ode 37 spreekt herinneren ons aan een motief dat
> meermalen in deze lideren naar vorenkomt: de
> moeiten (het woord is een hapax) zijn de pogingen
> van de dichter en de lof jegens God onder woorden to
> bringen, want de compositie van een loflied vereist
> vakmanschap, cf. Ode 16.

He suggests that in Ode 16 the Lord responds to the efforts of
the speaker to praise Him by sending His spirit which grants
the speaker the "fruits" of his labour:

> Ook het vakmanschap en de inspanningen van de
> dichter zijn opgenomen in Gods gnade, want vat tot
> uiting wordt gebracht zijn de vruchten die God
> geeft.

[11] See Ode 5.1 which duplicates Odes 16.3, but in the
reverse order.

[12] See the love language in Odes 3.2-9; 7.19; 8.1-22;
11.1,4; 12.1-13; 13.3; 14.3,6,7; 16.2,3; 18.1; 23.3; 40.4-6;
41.1-16; 42.3-9. For a discussion of these passages, see
Michael Lattke, _Einheit im Wort_. _Die spezifische Bedeutung_
von agapē, agapan, und philein im Johannesevangelium (SANT 41;
München: Kösel, 1975) 52-54.

[13] The phraseology is probably inspired by Ps 51.15.

[14] See also Odes 14.8, 6.1-2.

[15] E. Lohse, "_cheir_," _TDNT_ 9 (1974) 427, points out that
"God's action in history can be called the work of His hands
as creation can." See Is 5.12: ". . . but they do not regard
the deeds of the Lord or see the work of his hand," and Ps
111.7: "The works of his hands are faithful and just, all his
percepts are trustworthy."

[16] Lattke (121) translates vs 6b: "Und die Pflanzung
seiner Finger." A. F. J. Klijn in a review of Lattke's
edition of the Odes (_VC_ 34 [1980] 303) remarks, "This is not
impossible, but the Syriac has been translated by 'Dienst' in
16.2a. It is better to use the word 'work' in 16.6b." The
parallelism with `bd` also argues for the translation "labour"
or "work," whereas there is nothing in the context to support
preferring the secondary meaning, "planting."

[17] For a detailed study of the Odist's use of _mlt_', _ptgm_'
and possible links with Jn's use of _logos_, see James H.
Charlesworth, "Qumran, John and the Odes of Solomon," in _John_
and Qumran (ed. J. H. Charlesworth; London: Geoffrey Chapman,
1972) 106-136; "The Odes of Solomon and the Gospel of John,"
CBQ 35 (1973) 298-322; Jack T. Sanders, _The New Testament_
Christological Hymns (SNTSMS 15; Cambridge: University Press,
1971) 46ff, 101-120; Rudolf Bultmann, _Das Evangelium des_
Johannes (MeyerK Abt. 2; Göttingen: Vandenhoeck & Ruprecht,
1968) 5ff; C. H. Dodd, _The Interpretation of the Fourth Gospel_
(Cambridge: University Press, 1955) 273.

[18] Sebastian Brock, Review of Charlesworth, _JBL_ 93 (1974)
221.

[19] For a critique of Brock's proposal see Charlesworth,
"Haplography and Philology: A Study of Ode of Solomon 16.8,"
NTS 25 (1979) 221. Charlesworth notes that the scribe

responsible for Ms H was guilty of parablepsis twice in
copying vs 16.8 and corrects his errors by writing <u>bsy'</u> and <u>l'</u>
above the line. He argues that we should imagine an original
text reading:

> For the Word of the Lord investigates whatever is
>   invisible,
> And what is visible reveals the thought of the Lord.

At the conclusion of his complicated argument for restoring
the above line, he remarks, "Emendations and restorations are
naturally speculative and attractive primarily to those who
suggest them. . ." and he concedes, ". . . the thought may be
more created than restored" (226).

[20]See David Winston, <u>The Wisdom of Solomon</u> (AB 43; Garden
City: Doubleday, 1979) 180-81, 194; Dieter Georgi, <u>Weisheit
Salomos</u> (Gütersloh: Gerd Mohn, 1979) 47-48, 49. See also 1
Cor 2.9-13 where it is the Spirit who seems to fulfill this
task: "For the Spirit searches everything, even the depths of
God. . . ."

[21]Hans   Conzelmann,   <u>1   Corinthians</u>   (Hermeneia;
Philadelphia: Fortress Press, 1975) 63.

[22]Compare Rom 1.20: "For ever since the creation of the
world his invisible nature, namely, his eternal power and
deity, has been clearly perceived."

[23]Harris and Mingana (286) characterize the entire Ode in
the following way:

> This ode again belongs to the group of Wisdom-Odes;
> it is occupied with the praises of the Logos as the
> creative and providential instrument of God. All
> things were made by the Logos, and He was pre-
> existent before creation. The language is parallel
> to that of the first chapter of St. John's Gospel,
> but it also shows coincidences with Colossians and
> with Hebrews. . . .

Bernard likewise asserts: "This hymn is occupied with the
praises of the Word, and the agency of the word in creation
and nature" (80). As we will see, though both Jn and the
author of the Ode draw upon the Wisdom tradition, alluding to
the role of the Word in creation, the Odist stresses the
creative activity of God Himself, assigning to the Word and
the Thought at most a secondary significance, while in Jn 1
the Word is the center and theme of the prologue.

[24]Gunkel, "Die Oden Salomos," 327.

[25]Gen 2.2, Ex 31.17.

[26]They present as evidence Justin's <u>Dialogue with Trypho</u>
22, where Justin argues against the necessity of circumcision

and observance of the Sabbath, and a section from Gregory of Nyssa's The Testimonies against the Jews.

[27]H. M. Slee ("A Note on the Sixteenth Ode of Solomon," JTS [1914] 454) remarks:

> It appears from Philo's protest in De Migr Abr 16 that a thoughtful Jew could reflect on the unceasing activity of the heavenly bodies, and yet keep the Seventh Day; and this, in spite of the passage from Justin cited by Dr. Rendel Harris, seems to make it doubtful whether any anti-Judaic polemic is to be detected in this Ode.

F. Spitta ("Zum Verständnis der Oden Salomos.I," ZNW 11 [1910] 275) agrees: "Diese Ode 16 ist ganz jüdisch. Christliche Polemik gegen den Sabbath ist schon durch v.13 ausgeschlossen, aber auch sonst durch nichts angedeutet."

[28]J. A. Emerton, "Notes on Some Passages in the Odes of Solomon," JTS 28 (1977) 516.

[29]Emerton, "Notes," 516.

[30]Emerton, "Notes," 517.

[31]Emerton, "Notes," 517.

[32]Emerton, "Notes," 517. There is no reason to see here, as Harris and Mingana do (286), a reference to the teachings of Bardaisan, ". . . that the sun and moon exchanged illumination, the sun giving light to the moon when the latter is waxing and taking it back again when it is waning."

[33]Emerton, "Notes," 519.

[34]Emerton, "Notes," 517.

[35]Emerton, "Notes," 519.

[36]W. E. Crum, A Coptic Dictionary (Oxford: Clarendon, 1939) 36-37.

[37]See Hermann Sasse, "aiōn," TDNT 2 (1964) 97-209.

[38]See note 8; Aune, The Cultic Setting, 176, 180-184. See also Jannes Reiling, Hermas and Christian Prophecy (Leiden: Brill, 1973) 7-16; for the broader question of prophecy in the primitive Church see G. Dautzenberg, Urchristliche Prophetie: Ihre Erforschung, ihre Voraussetzungen im Judentum und ihre Struktur im ersten Korintherbrief (Stuttgart: Kohlhammer, 1979); E. Earle Ellis, Prophecy and Hermeneutic in Early Christianity (Grand Rapids: Eerdmanns, 1978); David Hill, New Testament Prophecy (Atlanta: John Knox, 1979); U. B. Müller, Prophetie und Predigt im Neuen Testament; Formgeschichtliche Untersuchungen zur urchristlichen Prophetie (Gütersloh: Gerd Mohn, 1979); Otto Michel,

"Spätjüdisches Prophetentum," in Neutestamentliche Studien für Rudolf Bultmann (ed. W. Eltester; Berlin: Töpelmann, 1957) 60-66.

[39]Aune, The Cultic Setting, 178.

[40]James M. Robinson "Die Hodajot-Formel im Gebet und Hymnus des Frühchristentums," in Apophoreta. Festschrift für Ernst Haenchen (ed. W. Eltester and F. W. Kettler; Berlin: Töpelmann, 1964) 213.

[41]For a discussion of the Spirit's role in the worship of the early Christian communities, see Rudolf Bultmann, Theology of the New Testament (trans. K. Grobel; New York: Charles Scribner's Sons, 1951) 1. 161. Bultmann notes:

> It (the common Christian conviction) understands everything that is given here as the gift of the Spirit, especially what transcends the limits of the ordinary - the word of instruction, which dispenses wisdom and knowledge, as well as prophecy, which uncovers the mystery of future events but which also reveals what lurks in the heart-prayers and songs and especially ecstatic speaking in tongues. (161)

See also Ferdinand Hahn, The Worship of the Early Church (trans. David E. Green; Philadelphia: Fortress Press, 1973) 44-46; Oscar Cullmann, Early Christian Worship (SBT 10; London: SCM, 1953) 35-36; Hermann Gunkel, Die Wirkungen des Heiligen Geistes (Göttingen: Vandenhoeck & Ruprecht, 1909) 71ff.

CHAPTER IV

[1]Gerhard Kittel, Die Oden Salomos, 26.

[2]John Michael LaFargue, Language and Gnosis: Form and Meaning in the Acts of Thomas ch 1-10 (Th.D. diss., Harvard Divinity School, 1977) 25-31, 183-197.

[3]Joachim Jeremias, "abyssos," TDNT 1 (1964) 9-10. See also Hans-Friedrich Weiss, Untersuchungen zur Kosmologie des hellenistischen und palästinischen Judentums (TU 97; Berlin: Akademie-Verlag, 1966) 12-17.

[4]Hans Conzelmann, ("skotos," TDNTI 7 [1971] 429) remarks, commenting on Gen 1.2: "From the very outset, then, darkness is connected with this primal flood."

[5]Conzelmann, "skotos," 428. See also Georg Fohrer, History of Israelite Religion (trans. David E. Green; Nashville: Abingdon, 1972) 219-200.

[6]John L. McKenzie, "Darkness," Dictionary of the Bible (Milwaukee: Bruce, 1965) 175.

[7]Heinz-Wolfgang Kuhn (Enderwartung und gegenwärtiges Heil [SUNT 4; Göttingen: Vandehoeck & Ruprecht, 1966] 54-55), expanding on the work of G. von Rad, described the Old Testament's understanding of the connection between the underworld and the earth, an understanding which the author of this Ode might well have inherited:

> Das Totenreich "manifestiert sich" überall da, zeigt
> "etwas von seinem Raum" wo immer der Tod regiert.
> Über alles, was "an Lebenskraft im weiteren Sinne
> arm ist," übt der Tod schon seine Herrschaft aus,
> und dort ist schon seine "Sphäre."

[8]Jörg Jeremias, Theophanie: die Geschichte einer alttestamentlicher Gattung (WMANT 10; Neukirchen: Vluyn, 1965) 108ff.

[9]George W. E. Nickelsburg, Jewish Literature Between the Bible and the Mishnah (Philadelphia: Fortress, 1981) 292.

[10]Harnack (63) insists that "the Lord" in vss 1-2 is "God Himself," whereas the singer in vss 3-5 is the Son. Kittel (Die Oden Salomos, 25) maintains, on the other hand, that Ode 31 ". . . schildert die Tätigkeit 'des Herrn' sicherlich des Messias, der deutlich vom Höchsten, seinem heiligen Vater (v. 4f) unterschieden ist." Abramowski, ("Der Christus der Salomooden," ZNW 35 [1936] 53) maintains that the title kyrios is applied to the Son in Odes 3, 7, 10, 17, 29, and here in Ode 31. R. Terzoli ("Repertorio dei nomi divini nelle Odi di Salomone," Vetera Christianorum 11 [1974] 130) contends that "Lord" in this Ode is to be identified with Christ.

[11]For a discussion of the dichotomies error-truth, ignorance-knowledge in Judaism, Christianity, and Gnostic myth, see James H. Charlesworth, "Qumran, John and the Odes," John and Qumran (ed. James H. Charlesworth; London: Geoffrey Chapman, 1972) 121-122, and Rudolf Bultmann, "Die Bedeutung der neuerschlossenen mandäischen und manichäischen Quellen für das Verständnis des Johannesevangeliums," ZNW 24 (1925) 112-113.

[12]Hermann Gunkel, "Die Oden Salomos," ZNW 11 (1910) 312.

[13]David E. Aune, The Cultic Setting of Realized Eschatology, 188, n.1.

[14]See Is 9.2, 16.6, 25.9, 44.23, 45.5, 49.13, 51.11, 61.7, 10, 65.14, 17, 66.10; Bar 4.22ff, 5.9; Zeph 3.14-17; Jl 2.21-27; Zech 2.14, 8.19, 9.9ff. See Hans Conzelmann, "chairo," TDNT 9 (1974) 363; Paul Volz, Die Eschatologie der jüdischen Gemeinde, 359ff; Rudolf Bultmann, "agalliaomai," TDNT 1 (1964) 20-21. In Qumran joy is of an eschatological character, though already realized: 1QM 1.9, 12.13, 13.12; 1QS 4.7; 1QH 13.6, 9.24ff. See Conzelmann ("chairō,") for the

uses of joy in the New Testament. Bultmann (Johannes, 387, n.1) remarks concerning the meaning of joy in the New Testament, ". . . doch gilt hier diese schon als gegenwärtig, ohne deshalb ihren eschatologischen Charakter zu verlieren. . . ."

[15]Conzelmann, "chairō," 362; Bultmann, Johannes, 387, n.1.

[16]Conzelmann, "chairō," 365-366.

[17]Conzelmann, "chairō," 371-372. Bultmann (Johannes, 387, n.1) sees joy as characteristic of what he calls "das gnostisierende Christentum" of Acts Thom., e.g., ch. 14, 142, 146, 148. See also the Gospel of Truth I 16, 31ff: "The Gospel of truth is a joy for those who have received from the Father of truth the gift of knowing him, through the power of the word that came forth from the pleroma."

[18]Hans Conzelmann, "charis," TDNT 9 (1974) 372-402.

[19]Raymond E. Brown, The Gospel According to John (AB 29; Garden City: Doubleday, 1966) 1. 14-15.

[20]See Pss 33.3, 40.4, 96.1, 144.9; Is 42.10; Rev. 5.19, 14.3.

[21]Our translation is based on the barely legible reading in N: db'ydh; H has db'ydwhy which would mean "those who were in his hands." In either case the masculine singular suffix could refer either to the Most High or to the subject.

[22]See Volz, Eschatologie, 394-395; Erich Sjöberg, "Wiedergeburt und Neuschöpfung im palästinischen Judentum," ST 4 (1951-52) 44-85.

[23]Raymond E. Brown (The Epistles of John [AB 30; Garden City: Doubleday, 1982] 390) describes how "these aspects of divine sonship/childhood . . . come to a focus in the community of the renewed Covenant at Qumran." See also Erich Sjöberg, "Neuschöpfung in den Toten-Meer Rollen," ST 9 (1956) 131-136; Kuhn, Enderwartung, 75ff.

[24]See 2 Cor 6.18; Rev 21.7; Lk 6.35; Mt 5.9; Heb 2.10; Gal 4.4-7; Jn 1.14; 3.3ff; 1 Jn 1.29, 3.1. For a discussion of New Testament texts which express the idea of Christians as children or sons of God or of receiving life from God, see Brown, Epistles, 384-389; Eduard Schweizer, "hyios," TDNT 8 (1972) 389-392.

[25]Bultmann, Johannes, 37. Bultmann (The Johannine Epistles [Hermeneia; trans. R. Philip O'Hara; Philadelphia: Fortress, 1973] 45-46) remarks:

Although the expression gennēthēnei ek tou theou ("born of God") is not attested in the same form in the mystery religions and Gnosticism, nevertheless, there can be no doubt that this manner of speaking,

i.e., the notion, born of God, derives from this
sphere.

Bultmann claims that both in Christian proclamation and in
Gnosticism the consciousness underlying such language ". . .
is that the old, natural man cannot without divine assistance,
attain the salvation to which he aspires, but that he requires
a renewal of his being." Brown (Epistles, 386) challenges
Bultmann's view and stresses the origin of the imagery in
Jewish apocalyptic:

> Rather the idea of the divine begetting of the
> Christian probably developed through an analogy
> based on eternal life. From intertestamental
> Judaism, which expressed the idea that God would
> give and (at times) had already given his select
> followers the life of the age to come . . .
> Johannine Christians developed the notion that the
> followers of Jesus already possessed this (eternal)
> life. This led to a comparison wherein, just as
> ordinary life is given by human begetting, eternal
> is given by divine begetting.

[26]Charlesworth ("Qumran," 128) sees in this verse similarities with John 17.1ff and wonders, "Is it possible that
the connection could be traced to the community from which the
Odes and John might have come?" Tsakona (545) also maintains
that Christ is presenting the saved, those who have become
sons through him to the Father, and cites Jn 17.6 and Heb
2.13. Jn 17, however, is not a presentation by Christ of the
saved, and is notably more "gnostic" than the rest of the
farewell discourse.

[27]Gunkel ("Die Oden," 312) recognizes the difficulty and
proposes that we emend the text to prswphwn, and translates
the line: "Sie wurden für gerecht erklärt."

[28]John Strugnell, oral suggestion.

[29]See Odes 3 and 41.

[30]Menard, L'Evangile de Vérité (NHS 2; Leiden: Brill,
1972) 73. See also Gottlob Schrenk, "patēr," TDNT 5 (1967)
978-979.

[31]See Gunkel, "Die Oden Salomos," Reden Und Aufsätze,
176; Abramowski, "Der Christus," 56; Bauer, 612; Schille, 49.

[32]Martin Dibelius and Hans Conzelmann, The Pastoral
Epistles (Hermeneia; trans. Philip Buttolph and Adela Yarbro;
Philadelphia: Fortress, 1972) 61. See also J. N. D. Kelly,
The Pastoral Epistles (Black's New Testament Commentaries;
London: Black, 1963) 90-91.

[33]Dibelius and Conzelmann, Pastoral Epistles, 62.

[34]Dibelius and Conzelmann, Pastoral Epistles, 62.

[35]Dibelius and Conzelmann, Pastoral Epistles, 62.

[36]Reginald Fuller, The Foundations of New Testament Christology (London: Lutterworth, 1965) 218. See also Joachim Jeremias, Die Briefe an Timotheus und Titus (NTD 9; Göttingen: Vandenhoeck & Ruprecht, 1963) 24: "Mit der Rechtfertigung könnte einem (freilich erst nachchristlich bezeugten) hellenistischen Sprachgebrauch gemäss, die Erhöhung in die Seinsweise der göttlichen Gerechtigkeit bezeichnet sein. . . ."

[37]See our discussion of the ascent of various redeemer figures in our study of Ode 36.

[38]Gunkel ("Die Oden" 176) for example, interprets the verse by paraphrasing it: ". . . kommt hervor, aus den Qualen des höllnerischen Kerkers." Gressmann (464) understands vs 6 as Christ's ". . . Aufforderung an die Gefangenen und Toten sich Freiheit und Leben anzueignen."

[39]Mt 26.63, 27.12,14; Mk 14.61, 15.5; Lk 23.9; 1 Pet 2.23.

[40]See Charlesworth, 117, n. 10 and G. R. Driver, "Notes on Two Passages in the Odes of Solomon," JTS 25 (1974) 436.

[41]Gunkel, "Die Oden," 176.

[42]Hennecke-Schneemelcher, 1.182. For a discussion of the origins and character of the text see Helmut Koester, Introduction 2.163.

[43]See Hans-Martin Schenke, "Die Tendenz der Weisheit zur Gnosis," Gnosis. Festschrift für Hans Jonas (ed. Barbara Aland; Göttingen: Vandenhoeck & Ruprecht, 1978) 361-364.

[44]George W. E. Nickelsburg, Resurrection, Immortality, and Eternal Life in Intertestamental Judaism (HTS 26; Cambridge: Harvard 1972) 48ff.

[45]Nickelsburg, Resurrection, 59.

[46]Nickelsburg, Resurrection, 58.

[47]Nickelsburg, Resurrection, 67.

[48]Nickelsburg, Resurrection, 87.

[49]Nickelsburg, Resurrection, 89.

[50]Dieter Georgi, "Der vorpaulinische Hymnus Phil 2, 6-11," Zeit und Geschichte. Dankesgabe an Rudolf Bultmann zum 80. Geburtstag. (ed. Erich Dinkler; Tübingen: J. C. B. Mohr, 1964) 272.

[51]Georgi, "Der vorpaulinische Hymnus," 274.

[52]Quoted in Jn 19.29; Mt 27.34,48; Mk 15.36; Lk 23.36. See Wolfgang Heidland, "oxos," TDNT 5 (1967) 288-289.

[53]He says of "the interpreters of falsehood and the seers of deceit": "And they stopped the thirsty from drinking the liquor of knowledge, and when they were thirsty they made them drink vinegar."

[54]Walter Grundmann, "tapeinos," TDNT 8 (1972) 11, notes:

> The LXX views the entire fate of the Servant as tapeinōsis and bears testimony: the tapeinōsis which he has taken on him removes judgement from him and is the reason for his exaltation full of salvation. This idea has its basis in the original Hebrew. What is summed up as tapeinōsis in the LXX is to be found in v. 7. The Servant of the Lord is mistreated and he submits.

See also Sir 2.2,5.

[55]G. J. Reinink, Review of Charlesworth in JSJ 5 (1974) 68.

[56]Brien McNeil, "The Odes of Solomon and the Sufferings of Christ," Symposium Syriacum, 1976 (Orientalia Christiana Analecta 205; Rome: Oriental Institute, 1978) 34.

[57]Charlesworth (117) translates ʾštwdyt as "I was promised," but the eshtaphal of ydʾ can only mean "I promised."

CHAPTER V

[1]Eduard Norden, Agnostos Theos. Untersuchungen zur Formengeschichte religiöser Rede (Darmstadt: Wissenschaftliche Buchgesellschaft, 1956).

[2]Similarly Beskow and Hidal remark: "Åter: Står i den syriska texten som här utan syftning" (68).

[3]Harnack likewise holds that twb in vs 1a and bh in vs 1b ". . . machen es wahrscheinlich, dass der Eingang fehlt" (64).

[4]See Hans Conzelmann, "charis," TDNT 9 (1974) 401-402; Rudolf Bultmann, Theology of the New Testament (trans. Kendrick Grobel; New York: Scribner's 1951) 1.156-159. The hypostatized figure of "grace" appears in a variety of gnostic texts. In the Valentinianism known to Irenaeus, "grace" is another name for the aeon "Ennoia," also called "Silence" (Adv.Haer. I.1.1). According to Irenaeus (Adv.Haer. I.12.1-3), "grace" is another name for the aeon "Silence" and plays a dominant role in the prayers of the Marcosians (e.g., "'May Grace who is before all things, who is beyond thought and description, fill thine inner man and multiply in thee her

knowledge, sowing the mustard seed in good soil.'" [Werner Foerster, Gnosis (trans. R. McL. Wilson: Oxford: Clarendon, 1972) I.201]). See also Ap. John (NHC II.1; 8, 3-4); Gos.Eg. (NHC III 2: 52, 9); Disc. 8-9 (NHC VI 6: 61, 3) and perhaps also Gos.Phil. (NHC II 3: 59, 5); Ap. Jas. (NHC i 2: 1,5); Treat. Res. (NHC I 4: 45, 13). H. J. W. Drijvers, ("Kerygma und Logos in den Oden Salomos dargestellt am Beispiel der 23. Ode," Kerygma und Logos. Festschrift für Carl Andresen [ed. Adolf Martin Ritter; Göttingen: Vandenhoeck & Ruprecht, 1979] 156) claims that tybwt³ in Ode 33.1 and 10, as well as in 9.5, 34.6, and 41.3 ". . . wird in den Oden für Gott verwendet und kann eben so ein Äquivalent des Christus sein." Ode 33, as we shall see, offers no conclusive evidence to support the identification of grace with either God or with Christ.

[5]Labourt (31) follows F. Schulthess ("Textkritische Bemerkungen zu den syrischen Oden Salomos," ZNW [1910] 255) in emending the text to read lbšt: "elle a revêtu la perdition," which renders the text even more mysterious.

[6]Harnack (64), for example, interprets bh as referring to "der Herr (Gott)," and Staerk and Ungnad maintain that it is the Messiah. It is not necessary, however, to introduce a new character into the poem at this point.

[7]Kittel (15) insists that it is Grace's activity which is being referred to throughout the Ode, even in vss 2-4. Bauer (613) queries, "Ist hier etwas in Unordnung, so dass man berechtigt wäre, mit H. Gressmann überall ein Femininum einzusetzen?" In any case, he concludes, "So, wie der Text heute lautet, muss wohl der Er der Erlöser sein, in dem die Sie, die Gnade oder Güte Gottes von oben herabkam." Erbetta (650) goes a step farther; not only does he identify the subject of vss 2-4 with a saviour figure, but he claims that

. . . su cui è scesa la grazia o la bontà divina, la cui opera, descritta all'inizio dell'ode, non è altro che quanto Cristo compì insieme ad essa. Potremmo pure pensare che la bontà del v. 1 supponga il gr. chrēstotēs, con evidente allusione a Cristo stesso, di cui termine farebbe le veci.

Bernard (117) considers the subject of vss 2-4 to be "Grace in the Person of Christ."

[8]G. J. Reinink, Review of Charlesworth in JSJ 5 (1972) 68. In Ode 38 the false Bridegroom and his Bride, perhaps representing a teacher and his church, who are regarded as heretical by the Odist, parody the Beloved and his Bride, in all likelihood, Christ and His church. In imitation of the Beloved and His Bride, the evil pair

. . . invite many to the wedding feast, And allow them to drink the wine of their intoxication (vs 12),

with the intention of leading them into error and of corrupting them.

[9]See Beskow and Hidal (46): "Det förintade fullständigt
inför sig." The construction resembles that of an infinitivus
absolutus, which, as Nöldeke puts it (225), ". . . dient dazu,
dem Verbum mehr Nachdruck zu geben, indem er die Handlung
einer anderen entgegensetzt oder ihre Intensivität ausdrückt."
Nöldeke explains that in Syriac an abstract noun corresponding
to the main verb can replace the infinitivus absolutus (226-
-227).

[10]For a study of Prv 8 see Gerhard von Rad, Wisdom in
Israel (Nashville: Abingdon, 1972) 149-166; R. B. Y. Scott,
Proverbs (AB 18; Garden City: Doubleday, 1956) 66-84.

[11]The Greek word for "proclaim," "say loudly" in the
passage in Jn is krazein, which Bultmann (Johannes, 50, n.3)
claims ". . . wird speziell vom inspirienten Reden gebraucht
. . ." See also Lk 1.41; Rom 8.15; Gal 4.6; Ign. Phld 7.1.

[12]See the discussion of Ulrich Wilckens, Weisheit und
Torheit. Eine exegetisch-religionsgeschichtliche Untersuchung
zu 1.Kor. 1 und 2 (BHT 26; Tübingen: J. C. B. Mohr, 1959)
138ff. He remarks vis-à-vis Ode 33.6-13: "Der zweite Teil
entspricht in seiner Form deutlich den Predigten der Weisheit
in der chokmatischen Literatur."

[13]As to the question of the origins of this type of
speech, Norden concedes, ". . . muss ich mich mit dem allge-
meinen Resultate 'mystisch-theosophische Literatur des
Orients' begnügen. (Agnostos Theos, 303) Norden describes
the use that was made of the mission speech:

> Propaganda im Dienst der gnosis theou ist das
> einigende Band gewesen, an dem die Missionare der
> verschiedensten Religionen . . . immer wieder
> dieselben Formen- und Gedankentypen in entsprech-
> enden Transformationen aufgereiht haben. (303)

[14]Norden, Agnostos Theos, 10.

[15]Norden shows how this "Selbstvorstellung" is employed
by Oriental deities and posits that the origin of this sort of
speech is to be found in the cult of the Oriental deities.
See Agnostos Theos 186, 207ff. As Thomas Arvedson (Das
Mysterium Christi. Eine Studie zu Mt 11.25-30 [Uppsala:
Wretmans, 1937] 90-91) notes:

> Der Redende stellt seine Identität fest, er legiti-
> iert sich. Aber die Selbstvorstellung des Gottes
> ist keineswegs nur eine Formalität. "Der unbekannte
> Gott" offenbart sich dadurch, dass er seinen Namen
> nennt. Er entfaltet sein Wesen.

See also Martin Dibelius, Die Formgeschichte des Evangeliums
(Tübingen: J. C. B. Mohr, 1933) 282: "Die Verbindung von
Selbstempfehlung und Predigtaufruf ist das typische Kenn-
zeichen des göttlichen oder halbgöttlichen Offenbarungsträgers

in der hellenistischen Frömmigkeit, also einer mythischen Person."

[16]See Norden's study of the term in Agnostos Theos, 134-140 and J. Behm, "metanoeō," TDNT 4 (1967) 978-980, 989-1008.

[17]Wilckens (Weisheit und Torheit, 138) notes, "Der Ruf zur Umkehr ist für die Gattung der Weisheitspredigten wie überhaupt für die jüdische weisheitliche Mahnrede typisch."

[18]Commenting on this verse, Bultmann (Johannes, 228, n.7) remarks, "Der Ruf erchesthō (pros me) ist der typische Ruf des Heilbringers und Offenbarers." See also Ode 30.1, 21.6; Mt 11.28.

[19]For possible uses and applications of this motif by the Elchasaites, the author of the Ps. Clementine Homilies and in Manichaean texts, see the discussion in David Winston, The Wisdom of Solomon (AB 43; Garden City: Doubleday, 1979) 188.

[20]Wilckens, Weisheit und Torheit, 138-139.

[21]Norden (Agnostos Theos, 7, n.1) claims, in regard to Ode 33.8c, "Gemeint war in dem vom Verf. reproduzierten Original sicher die gnōsis; während er diesen Begriff in anderen Oden beibehält, hat er ihn hier durch 'weise machen' und 'Wege der Wahrheit' judaisiert (vgl. Gressmann S. 9)." There is no indication, however, that gnosis ever stood in the original of this Ode, nor is there reason to think that an editor "judaized" the original.

[22]Here too Wisdom may stand in the background, for as Arvedson (Mysterium, 163-194) points out, "Wer sich der Weisheit hingibt, bekommt reichen Lohn. Sie ist der beste der Schätze, bzw, schenkt grossen Reichtum, sie gibt Trost, Freude, und Genuss, Gesundheit, Ruhe, Frieden und Sicherheit, Schutz, Ehre. Vor allem aber gibt sie Leben." See Prv 2.11-22, 3.16, 7.2, 8.35ff, 9.6; Sir 1.8, 4.12, 6.28, 14.27, 15.4; Wis 8.9, 16, 9.11.

[23]See Hermann Sasse, "aiōn," TDNT 1 (1964) 204-207.

[24]For the connotation of eschatological salvation, see J. Behm, "kainos," TDNT 3 (1965) 449-450: "Kainos is the epitome of the wholly different and miraculous thing which is brought about by the time of salvation." See, for example, 2 Cor 5.17: "When anyone is united to Christ, there is a new creation; the old order has gone, and a new order has already begun." See Hans Windisch, Der zweite Korintherbrief (MeyK Abt. 6; ed. Georg Strecker; Göttingen: Vandenhoeck & Ruprecht, 1970) 189-191.

[25]l' hbl' is regularly used to translate aphtharsia, and hbl' for diaphthora; see Payne Smith, 1179-1180. See also Günther Harder, "phtheirō," TDNT 9 (1974) 93-106.

^{26}Hans Dieter Betz, _Galatians_ (Hermeneia; Philadelphia: Fortress, 1979) 187.

^{27}Betz (_Galatians_, 188) cites numerous texts where "putting on" a redeemer figure is used in mystery religions. The term is also frequently found in gnostic literature, e.g., ActsThom. 108-113; Gos.Thom. 36-37; Gos.Phil. 24; Gos.Truth 20.30ff; Thom.Cont. 143.37.

^{28}Betz (_Galatians_, 188) distinguishes between "putting on Christ" in baptism (Gal 3.27; Col 3.10; Eph 4.24; Gos.Phil. [NHC II 75: 21-25]), as a phrase used in parenesis (Rom 13.12, 14; Col 2.12, 3.9ff; Eph 4.22-24, 6.11, 14; 1 Thess 5.8), and as a hope to be realized in the hereafter (1 Cor 15.53ff; 2 Cor 5.3; Rev 15.6, 19.14).

^{29}Betz, _Galatians_, 187.

^{30}Gottfried Quell, "eklegomai," _TDNT_ 4 (1967) 145-168.

^{31}Quell, "eklegomai," 171-172.

^{32}Quell, "eklegomai," 183-185.

^{33}Gottlob Schrenk, "eklektos," _TDNT_ 4 (1967) 186-192.

^{34}In Jn Jesus is the one who elects, and always in solemn "I" statements: 6.70, 13.18, 15.16, 19. The call and election of the perfect virgin, however, is unlike that of Jesus in Jn; it is not an election of the chosen from out of the world. See Rudolf Bultmanmn, _Johannes_, 419, n.2.

^{35}For "walking" as an image of man's religious and moral life in the Old Testament and early Christian literature, see Georg Bertram and Heinrich Seesemann, "pateō," _TDNT_ 5 (1967) 940-945. See also Hans Conzelmann, _Der Brief an die Kolosser_ (NTD 8; Göttingen: Vandenhoeck & Ruprecht, 1970) 143.

^{36}C. F. D. Moule, _The Epistle to the Colossians and to Philemon_ (Cambridge: University Press, 1958) 90.

^{37}See also Sir 15.2, 51.26; Philo Congr. 123; Fug. 141; Ebr. 145. The language of love and references to union can be found throughout Wisdom literature. In analyzing vss 12 and 13 Arvedson (_Mysterium Christi_, 171) concedes that Wisdom uses the language of "mystische Einheit mit der Göttin," but he sees a further development in Ode 33's use of the motif:

> Die mystische Betrachtungsweise, deren erste Keime wir in der Weisheitsliteratur beobachteten, hat sich hier durchsetzt und die alten Ausdrucksformen völlig durchtränkt. Die Kühnheit der Bildersprache und die Sicherheit und Selbstverständlichkeit, womit die mystischen Termini verwendet werden, setzen eine lange Entwicklung voraus. Dort hatten wir die ersten tastenden Ansätze, hier sind wir am Ende des Weges. Die Weisheit ist zu Gnosis geworden.

Wilckens (Weisheit und Torheit, 135) also claims, "Wir haben
es daher, religionsgeschichtlich gesehen, mit einem wichtigen
Zwischenglied zwischen jüdischer und gnostischer Sophia-Lehre
zu tun." See, however, the important article of R. A.
Horsley, "Spiritual Marriage with Sophia," VC 33 (1979) 30-54.
For the development of the theme in the Syrian tradition, see
R. Graffin, "Recherches sur le thème de l'Eglise-Epouse dans
les liturgies et la littérature patristique de langue
syriaque," OrSyr 3 (1958) 317-336; Jeanne-Ghislaine Van
Overstraeten, "Les liturgies nuptiales des églises de langue
syriaque et le mystère de l'Eglise-Epouse," Parole de L'Orient
8 (1977-78) 235-311.

[38]Hans Bietenhard, "onoma," TDNT 5 (1967) 242-281. See
also the important use of onoma in Jn 3.18, 17.6, 11, 12,
where, however, the name belongs not to the revealer but to
the Father. For John's use of onoma see Bultmann, Johannes,
327.6, 380-381.

[39]See the literature cited in note 49 to our study of Ode
36.

[40]Because he takes vss 2-4 to refer to the redeemer
mentioned in vs 1, Wilckens (Weisheit und Torheit, 136-137)
sees the redeemer figure in Ode 33 as a syzygy, such as we
find among the Valentinians:

> Wir sahen - besonders deutlich bei den Gnostikern
> des Irenäus - wie nach der Vereinigung des Erlösers
> mit der Sophia beide zusammen, in einer Syzygie
> vereint, zur Lösung der Pneumatiker herabkommen. In
> dieser Syzygie sind sie beide den zu erlösenden
> Pneumatikern gegenüber eines. Diese vorvalentinian-
> ische Vorstellung erklärt m.E. besser die Austausch-
> barkeit des männlichen und weiblichen Subjektes in
> der Ode. Die "Güte" Gottes ist hier ja selbst als
> eine Person vorgestellt, die jedoch den Angeredeten
> gegenüber mit der Person des (männlicher) Erlösers
> identisch ist.

Helmut Koester (Review of Wilckens in Gnomon 33 [1961] 594)
shows far greater understanding of the text and of the religious background of the Odes when he remarks:

> In Od Sal. 33 ist der Wechsel von 'er' und 'sie'
> ebenfalls kein Beleg für die behauptete Syzygien-
> Identität, sondern ein Anzeichen dafür, dass hier
> wie überhaupt in den Oden disparate Elemente eklekt-
> isch in der Mystik verwoben sind.

[41]See Antonio Orbe's study of "El Espíritu Virginal" in
his La Teología del Espíritu Santo. Estudios Valentinianos
Vol. IV (Analecta Gregoriana 158; Rome: Gregorian University,
1966) 43-68.

[42]Günther Bornkamm, Mythos und Legende in den apokryphen Thomas-Akten (Göttingen: Vandenhoeck & Ruprecht, 1933) 82-103.

[43]Günther Bornkamm, "The Acts of Thomas," New Testament Apocrypha (2 vols.; ed. E. Hennecke and W. Schneemelcher; English translation editor R. McL. Wilson; Philadelphia: Westminster 1963-65) 2.438.

[44]Bornkamm, "The Acts of Thomas," 439. See also his remarks in Mythos und Legende, 99:

So viel hier auch sprachlich unsicher ist, und so mannigfach die in den Epiklesen auf die mētēr gesammelten Züge in den verschiedenen Systemen auf verschiedene Gestalten verteilt sein mögen, an der Benennung der Erlösergöttin als "Jungfrau" ist kein Zweifel.

[45]Bornkamm, Mythos und Legende, 94-95.

[46]For a discussion of the elements of the gnostic redeemer myth, see our discussion of Ode 36 and the literature cited in notes 32-34 of that study. Wilckens (Weisheit und Torheit, 138), who is convinced of the gnostic character of the Ode, nonetheless concedes,

Allerdings darf man nun auch nicht übersehen, dass wesentliche Züge des gnostischen Mythos hier fehlen: So vor allem das Pleroma über dem Erlöser, besonders der gnostische Urvater. Es fällt kein Wort darüber, dass er die Seinen hinweg- und hinaufführt.

[47]For a study of the Holy Spirit in gnostic literature, see, in addition to the work of Orbe cited in note 39, R. McL. Wilson, "The Spirit in gnostic literature," Christ and Spirit in the New Testament. In Honour of C. F. D. Moule (ed. Barnabas Lindars and Stephen S. Smalley; Cambridge: University Press, 1973) 345-355. For a discussion of the Spirit as feminine, see Robert Murray, Symbols of Church and Kingdom. A Study in Early Syriac Tradition (Cambridge: University Press, 1975) 142-144, 312-320. See also Winfrid Cramer, Der Geist Gottes und des Menschen in frühsyrischer Theologie (Münsterische Beiträge zur Theologie, 46; Münster: Aschendorff, 1979); Georg Kretschmar, Studien zur frühchristlichen Trinitätslehre (BHT 21; Tübingen: J. C. B. Mohr, 1956) 21ff, 57ff. For an overview of the role of the Holy Spirit in biblical and intertestamental literature, see C. F. D. Moule, The Holy Spirit (Grand Rapids: Eerdmans, 1978); Eduard Schweizer, The Holy Spirit (trans. Reginald H. and Ilse Fuller; Philadelphia: Fortress, 1978); Hermann Gunkel, Die Wirkungen des heiligen Geistes (Göttingen: Vandenhoeck & Ruprecht, 1909).

CHAPTER VI

[1]See, for example, David E. Aune, The Cultic Setting of
Realized Eschatology in Early Christianity (NovTSup 28;
Leiden: Brill, 1972) 190: "The Odes of Solomon constitute a
homogenous collection of Christian hymns put into final form
by a single author-editor." Aune does not explain exactly
what he means by "homogenous," nor does he advert again in his
study to the activity of the "single author-editor" who is
responsible for the collection in its final form. Indeed, he
never addresses the question of the purpose of the final
collection. If by "homogenous" he means a unity of style,
that unity of style can be explained without having to posit a
single author or editor.

[2]Hans-Wolfgang Kuhn, Enderwartung und gegenwärtiges Heil
(SUNT: Göttingen: Vandenhoeck & Ruprecht, 1966) 26.

[3]Elizabeth Schüssler Fiorenza ("Wisdom Mythology and
Christological Hymns of the New Testament," Aspects of Wisdom
in Judaism and Early Christianity [ed. Robert L. Wilken:
Notre Dame: University of Notre Dame, 1975] 32) points out,
for example, that while we can isolate elements common to both
Jewish Wisdom and gnostic mythology, these common elements
". . . have different functions in their respective
theological contexts and these differences are of decisive
importance."

[4]The attitude with which Joachim Schüpphaus (Die Psalmen
Salomos [ALGHJ 7; Leiden: Brill, 1977] 19) treats the Psalms
of Solomon should be employed in studying the Odes:

> Ferner ist klar geworden, dass der theologische
> Zusammenhang nur von den Psalmen selbst entfaltet
> werden kann in enger Orientierung an den einzelnen
> Texten und unter dem Verzicht, sie sogleich in ein
> bestimmtes dogmatisches Koordinatensystem pressen zu
> wollen.

[5]See, for example, Riccardo Terzoli's (Il Tema della
Beatitudine nei Padri Siri [Brescia: Morcelliana, 1972]
19-20) comments on Ode 11: "Colpisce immediatemente il fatto
che il paradiso non è visto come la sede dell'uomo dopo la
morte e la resurrezione; l'autore dell'inno afferma esplica-
mente di essere già entrato in esso." He remarks on the
eschatology of the Odes:

> Qui la vita, la liberazione e l'incorruttibilità
> (insieme alla luce ed alla gioia) sono indicate come
> gli effetti dell'incontro con il Signore. Tutte le
> espressioni sono atemporali, ma è evidente che
> l'autore si riferisce alla sua situazione personale;
> e si può dire perciò che tali realità divine ed
> escatologiche sono già attualmente presenti.

[6]For a discussion of lifting up of hands and stretching
out of arms as gestures of petition and as normal postures for

prayer see Tj. Baarda, "'Het Uitbreiden Van Handen Is Zijn
Teke,'" Loven en Geloven Opstellen van collegas en medewerkers
aangeboden aan Prof. Dr. Nic. H. Ridderbos ter gelegenheid van
zijn vijfentuintigjarig ambstjubileum als hoosgeleraar ann de
Vrije Universiteit to Amsterdam (ed. Ton Bolland; Amsterdam:
Voorheen H. A. van Bottenburg, 1978) 250ff.

[7] As Wolfgang Langbrandtner (Weltferner Gott oder Gott der
Liebe [Beiträge zur biblischen Exegese und Theologie 6;
Frankfurt: Peter Lang, 1977] 158) puts it: "Diese Wieder-
geburt bedeutet die Inbesitznahme der Nature Gottes, da der
Glaubende nach dessen Vorbild umgestaltet wird, obwohl er noch
Mensch ist."

[8] "Garment of glory" and the equivalent term "garment of
light" were favorite motifs in the Jewish tradition, especially the apocrypha and pseudepigraphical writings, and in
the texts of early Christianity, particularly those representative of the Syrian tradition. For a thorough study of this
imagery and its background see A. Kowalski, "'Rivestiti di
gloria'. Adamo ed Eva nel commento di S. Efrem a Gen 2.25
(Ricerca sulle fonti dell'esegesi siriaca)," Cristianismo
nella Storia 3 (1982) 41-60. For the rich and extremely
important history of the use of light imagery, see Rudolf
Bultmann, "Zur Geschichte der Lichtsymbolik im Altertum,"
Philologus 97 (1948) 1-36; Carsten Colpe, "Lichtsymbolik in
alten Iran und antiken Judentum," Studium Generale 18 (1965)
116ff; Hans Conzelmann, "phōs," TDNT 9 (1974) 310-358; G.
Filoramo, "Pneuma e luce in alcuni testi gnostici," August-
inianum (1980) 595-614; S. Aalen, Die Begriffe 'Licht' und
'Finsternis' im Alten Testament, im Spätjudentum und im
Rabbinismus (Oslo: Kommisjon Hos Jacob Dybuad, 1951).

[9] P. Vielhauer, ("'Anapausis' Zum gnostischen Hintergrund
des Thomas-Evangeliums," Apophoreta, Festschrift für Ernst
Haenchen [ed. W. Eltester, F. H. Kettler; Berlin: Töpelmann,
1964] 291) observes that the concept of rest as realized in
the present appears primarily in those Odes which he judges to
be dealing with ascent, Odes 35, 36, 38, and in those which
emphasize loving union with the saviour, Odes 3, 38, 42. In
his judgement both represent mystical-ecstatic phenomena which
have the same result: the transformation of the Odist into a
heavenly state-of-being in which he enjoys true and lasting
peace and rest. Both rest and peace are found in such abundance in texts which describe future eschatological salvation,
that Paul Volz (Die Eschatologie der judischen Gemeinde
[Tübingen: J. C. B. Mohr, 1934] 347) remarks, "So kann die
Seligkeit selbst als 'Ruhe,' das Seligwerden als ein 'zur Ruhe
kommen' bezeichnet werden." See, e.g., Wis 3.3, 4.7, 5.16;
Esr 7.13,36,123, 8.52; Enoch 1.8, 5.7, 105.2; T. Dan 5; T.
Levi 18; Bar 85.9, 89.11. The Odist's use of rest in the Odes
of Ascent has nothing to do with the anapausis speculation
which we find in Philo and which is incorporated in Gnostic
literature.

[10]J. A. Emerton, "Some Problems of Text and Language in the Odes of Solomon," JTS 18 (1967) 373-374.

[11]Roger Le Déaut, "Le Thème de la Circoncision du Coeur," Congress Volume, Vienna, 1980 (VTSup 32; Leiden: Brill, 1981) 197-198.

[12]For a careful study of the history and development of the imagery of the cloud, see J. Luzarraga, Las Tradiciones de la Nube en la Biblia y en Judaismo Primitivo (AnBib 54; Rome: Biblical Institute, 1973).

[13]Luzarraga, Las Tradiciones, 113ff.

[14]Luzarraga, Las Tradiciones, 235-236; see also G. Martelet, "Sacrements, figure et exhortation en 1 Cor., x.1-11," RSR 44 (1956) 336ff. Among the New Testament texts, see, e.g., Jn 1613, 17.22; Rom 8.14, 9.4; 1 Cor 10.2; 1 Pet 4.14; Acts 1.5, 2.2.

[15]Luzarraga, Las Tradiciones, 129, n.484.

[16]G. Herzog-Hauser ("Milch," PW 15 [1932] 1578-79) traces the use and significance of milk in the Hellenistic mystery cults, from which he ⁻suggests, Christianity borrowed the custom of giving milk and honey to the newly baptized. Leonhard Goppelt (Der Erste Petrusbrief [MeyerK 12.1; Göttingen: Vandenhoeck & Ruprecht, 1978] 134) maintains that the mysteries and magic provide the background for the use of milk imagery in the Odes:

> Hier ist das symbolische Trinken von Milch, durch
> das in den Mysterien und im Zauber Anteil am Gött-
> lichem dargestellt, oder vermittelt wird, Bild für
> die eigentliche Nahrung geworden, die in dualist-
> ischer Antithese zur uneigentlichen steht.

See Heinrich Schlier, "gala," TDNT 1 (1964) 647, who posits that the notion of milk as a sacramental element that trans-mitted life passed over into gnosticism as the mysterious sacramental means of salvation.

[17]According to the analysis of Langbrandtner (Weltferner Gott, 157):

> Die Gaben, die er von Gott bei seiner Gemeinschaft
> mit ihm erhält, umschreibt der Verfasser mit "Milch"
> und "Tau", womit wahrscheinlich, wie aus anderen
> Stellen hervorgeht, die Offenbarung gemeint ist, die
> er in vollem Umfang erhält und die ihm "Ruhe"
> verleiht (35.6), den höchsten Grad der gnostischen
> Vollkommenheit. Diese Gemeinschaft zu Glaubendem
> und Gott nennt die Ode in v. 7 Himmelfahrt der
> Seele, die der Dichter als ein sich Ausrichten auf
> Gott hin, das die Erlösung zur Folge hat (35.7)
> versteht.

[18]See the reference to the "Helper," paraklētos, in Jn
14.16, where he is identified as the "Spirit of Truth," and in
16.25: "The Helper, the Holy Spirit, whom the father will
send in my name, he will teach you all things." See Ernest
Bammel, "Jesus und der Paraklet in Johannes 16," Christ and
Spirit in the New Testament. In Honor of C.F.D. Moule (ed.
Barnabas Lindars, Stephen S. Smalley; Cambridge University,
1973) 199-217; see also Bultmann's excursus on the Paraclete
in Johannes, 437-441, and Raymond E. Brown (The Gospel According to John, 2.710-717) who traces the roots of the paraclete
figure back to antecedents in Wisdom literature.

[19]E. g., Bernard, 68.

[20]For the history of the Descensus ad Inferos motif, and
especially its use in the Christian tradition, see: A.
Grillmeier, "Höllenabstieg," LTK 5 (1960) 450-455; "Der
Gottessohn im Totenreich," ZKT 71 (1949) 1-53, 184-203; H. F.
Vogels, Christi Abstieg ins Totenreich und das Läuterungs-
gericht an den Toten. Eine bibeltheologische-dogmatische
Untersuchung zum Glaubensartikel "descendit ad inferos"
(Freiburger Theologische Studien 102; Freiburg: Herder,
1976); W. Maas, Gott und die Hölle. Studien zum Descensus
Christi (Coll. Sammlung Horizonte, Neue Folge 14; Einsiedeln:
Johannesverlag, 1979); M. Peel, "The 'Descensus Ad Inferos' in
'The Teachings of Silvanus' (CG VII, 4)," Numen 26 (1982)
23-49.

BIBLIOGRAPHY

For a thorough bibliography on the Odes of Solomon up to 1971, see J. H. Charlesworth, The Odes of Solomon, cited below.

Aalen, S. Die Begriffe "Licht" und "Finsternis" im Alten Testament, im Spätjudentum und im Rabbinismus. Oslo: Jacob Dybwad, 1951.

Abramowski, R. "Der Christus der Salomooden." JTS 35 (1936) 44-69.

Adam, A. "Die ursprüngliche Sprache der Salomooden," ZNW 52 (1961) 141-156.

Arvedson, Thomas. Das Mysterium Christi. Eine Studie zu Mt 11.25.30. Uppsala: Wretmans, 1937.

Aune, David E. The Cultic Setting of Realized Eschatology in Early Christianity. NTS Supplements 28. Leiden: Brill, 1972.

_____. "The Odes of Solomon and Early Christianity." Society of New Testament Studies Meeting, Toronto, August, 1981.

Baarda, Tj. "'Het Uitbreiden van mijn handen is zijn teken' Enkele notities bij de gebedshouding in de Oden van Salomo." In Loven en geloven. Opstellen van collegas en medewerkers aangeboden aan Prof. Dr. Nic. H. Ridderbos ter gelegeheid van zijn vijfentuitigjarig ambstjubileum als hoosgeleraar aan de Vrije Universiteit Amsterdam. Ed. Ton Bolland. Amsterdam: Voorheen H. A. Bottenburg, 1978, 244-259.

Bammel, Ernest. "Jesus und der Paraklet in Johannes 16." In Christ and Spirit in the New Testament. In Honour of C. F. D. Moule. Ed. Barnabas Lindars, Stephen S. Smalley. Cambridge: Cambridge University, 1973, 199-217.

Barrett, C. K. The Gospel According to St. John: An Introduction with Commentary and Notes on the Greek Text. 2nd ed. Philadelphia: Westminster, 1978.

Bauer, W. Die Oden Salomos. KlT 64. Berlin: de Gruyter, 1933.

_____. Die Briefe des Ignatius von Antiochia und der Polykarpbrief. HNT Ergänzungsband. Die apostolischen Väter 2. Tübingen: J. C. B. Mohr, 1920.

Baumgartner, W. "Das trennende Schwert. Oden Salomos 28:
    4." In Festschrift Alfred Bertolet zum 80. Geburtstag.
    Ed. W. Baumgartner and L. Rost. Tubingen: J. C. B.
    Mohr, 1950, 50-57.

Behm, J. "kainos." TDNT 3 (1965) 449-450.

_____. "metanoeō." TDNT 4 (1967) 978-1008.

Bernard, D. A. Rev. of Die Oden Salomos, by Michael Lattke.
    RHPR 61 (1981) 282-283.

Bernard, J. H. The Odes of Solomon. TextsS 8.3. Cambridge:
    University Press, 1912.

Betz, Hans Dieter. Galatians. Hermeneia. Philadelphia:
    Fortress, 1979.

_____. Lukian von Samosata und das Neue Testament. TU 76.
    Berlin: Akademie-Verlag, 1961.

Beyer, Klaus. "Der reichsaramäische Einschlag in der ältesten
    syrischen Literatur." ZDMG 116 (1966) 242-254.

Bianchi, Ugo. "Questioni storico-religiose relative al
    Cristianesimo in Siria nei secoli II-V." Augustinianum
    19 (1979) 41-52.

Bieder, W. Die Vorstellung von der Höllenfahrt Jesu Christi.
    ATANT 19. Zürich: Zwingli-Verlag, 1949.

Bietenhard, Hans. Die Himmlische Welt im Urchristentum und
    Spätjudentum. WUNT 2. Tübingen: J. C. B. Mohr, 1951.

_____. "onoma." TDNT 5 (1967) 242-281.

Black, Matthew. Rev. of The Odes of Solomon, by J. H.
    Charlesworth. ExpTim 85 (1973) 217ff.

Bornkamm, Günther. Mythos und Legende in den apokryphen
    Thomas-Akten. Göttingen: Vandenhoeck & Ruprecht, 1933.

Bousset, Wilhelm. "Die Himmelsreise der Seele." ARW 4 (1901)
    136-169, 229-273.

_____. Die Religion des Judentums im späthellenistischen
    Zeitalter. HNT 21. Tübingen: J. C. B. Mohr, 1926.

_____. Kyrios Christos. Trans. John E. Steely.
    Nashville: Abingdon, 1970.

Brioso Sanchez, Maximo. Aspectos y Problemas del Himno
    Cristiano Primitivo. Theses et Studia Philologica
    Salamanticensia 17. Salamanca: Consejo Superior de
    Investigaciones Cientificas, Colegio Trilinguë de la
    Universidad, 1972.

Brock, S. P. Rev. of The Odes of Solomon, by J. H.
    Charlesworth. BSOAS 38 (1975) 142-143.

_____. Rev. of The Odes of Solomon, by J. H. Charlesworth.
    JBL 93 (1974) 623-625.

Brown, Raymond E. The Epistles of John. AB 30. Garden City:
    Doubleday, 1982.

_____. The Gospel According to John 2 vols. AB 29, 29A.
    Garden City: Doubleday, 1966, 1970.

Braun, F. M. "L'Enigme des Odes de Salomon." Rev Thom 57
    (1957) 597-603.

Bruston, C. Les plus anciens cantiques chrétiens. Paris:
    Librairie Fischbacher, 1912.

Bultmann, Rudolf. "agalliaomai." TDNT 1 (1964) 20-21.

_____. Das Evangelium des Johannes. MeyerK Abt. 2.
    Göttingen: Vandenhoeck & Ruprecht, 1968.

_____. "Die Bedeutung der neuerschlossenen mandäischen und
    manichäischen Quellen fur das Verständnis des Johannes-
    evangelium." ZNW 24 (1925) 100-147.

_____. "Ein jüdisch-christliches Psalmbuch aus dem ersten
    Jahrhundert." Monatschrift für Pastoraltheologie 7
    (1910) 23-29.

_____. Primitive Christianity. Trans. R. H. Fuller.
    Cleveland: Meridian, 1956.

_____. The Johannine Epistles. Hermeneia. Trans. R.
    Philip O'Hara. Philadelphia: Fortress, 1973.

_____. Theology of the New Testament. Trans. K. Grobel.
    New York: Charles Scribner's Sons, 1951.

_____. "Zur Geschichte der Lichtsymbolik im Altertum."
    Philologus 97 (1948) 1-36.

Burkitt, F. C. "A New Ms of the Odes of Solomon." JTS 13
    (1912) 372-385.

Carmignac, J. "Les affinités qumrâniennes de la onzième Ode
    de Salomon." RevQ 3 (1961) 71-102.

_____. "Recherches sur la langue originelle des Odes de
    Salomon." RevQ 4 (1963) 429-432.

_____. "Un qumrânien converti au christianisme: l'auteur
    des Odes de Salomon." In Qumran-Probleme. Ed. H.
    Bardtke. Berlin: Akademie-Verlag, 1963, 75-108.

Chadwick, H.   "Some Reflections on the Character and Theology
     of the Odes of Solomon."   In Kyriakon, Festschrift
     Johannes Quasten. Ed. P. Granfield and J. A. Jungmann.
     Munster: Aschendorff, 1970, 266-270.

Charlesworth, J. H.   "b'wt' in Earliest Christianity."   In The
     Use of The Old Testament in the New and Other Essays:
     Studies in Honour of William Franklin Stinespring.   Ed.
     J. M. Efird.   Durham, N.C.:   Duke University, 1972,
     271-279.

_____.   "Haplography and Philology: A Study of Ode of
     Solomon 16.8."   NTS 25 (1979) 221-227.

_____.   "Les Odes de Salomon et les manuscrits de la Mer
     Morte."   RB 77 (1970) 522-549.

_____ and R. A. Culpepper.   "Odes of Solomon and the Gospel
     of John."   CBQ 35 (1973) 298-322.

_____.   Papyri and Leather Manuscripts of the Odes of
     Solomon.   Dickerson Series of Facsimilies of Manuscripts
     Important for Christian Origins 1.   Durham, N.C.:   Duke
     University, 1981.

_____.   "Paronomasia and Assonance in the Syriac Text of
     the Odes of Solomon."   Semitics 1 (1970) 12-26.

_____.   "Qumran, John and the Odes of Solomon."   In John
     and Qumran.   Ed. J. H. Charlesworth.   London: Geoffrey
     Chapman, 1972, 107-136.

_____.   The Odes of Solomon.   SBLTT 13.   Missoula:
     Scholars, 1977.

_____.   "The Odes of Solomon and the Gospel of John."   CBQ
     35 (1973) 298-322.

_____.   "The Odes of Solomon - Not Gnostic."   CBQ 31 (1969)
     357-369.

_____.   The Pseudepigrapha and Modern Research.   SBLSCS 7.
     Missoula: Scholars, 1976.

Collins, John J.   "The Apocalyptic Technique: Setting and
     Function in the Book of Watchers."   JBL 44 (1982) 91-111.

_____.   The Apocalyptic Vision of the Book of Daniel.   HSM
     16.   Missoula: Scholars, 1977.

Colpe, Carsten.   "Der erlöste Erlöser."   Der Islam 32 (1957)
     195-214.

_____.   "Die Himmelsreise der Seele."   In Le Origini dello
     Gnostismo: Colloquio di Messina, 13-18 Aprile, 1966;

Testi e Discussioni.   Ed. Ugo Bianchi.   Supplements to
Numen 12. Leiden: Brill, 1967, 429-445.

_____. Die religionsgeschichtliche Schule: Darstellung
und Kritik ihrer Bilder vom gnostischen Erlösermythus.
FRLANT 78. Göttingen: Vandenhoeck & Ruprecht, 1961.

_____. "New Testament and Gnostic Christology."   In
Religions in Antiquity.   Essays in Memory of E. R.
Goodenough.   Ed. Jacob Neusner.   Leiden: Brill, 1968,
230-237.

Connolly, R. H. "Greek the Original Language of the Odes of
Solomon." JTS 14 (1913) 250-262.

Conybeare, F. C. "The Odes of Solomon Montanist." ZNW 12
(1911) 70-75.

Conzelmann, Hans. "chairō." TDNT 9 (1974) 359-372.

_____. "charis." TDNT 9 (1974) 373-402.

_____. 1 Corinthians. Hermeneia. Trans. James W. Leitch.
Philadelphia: Fortress, 1975.

_____. Der Brief an die Kolosser. NTD 8. Göttingen:
Vandenhoeck & Ruprecht, 1970.

_____. "phōs." TDNT 9 (1974) 310-358.

_____. "skotos." TDNT 7 (1971) 423-445.

Corwin, Virginia. St. Ignatius and Christianity in Antioch.
New Haven: Yale, 1960.

Cramer, Wilfrid.   Der Geist Gottes und des Menschen im
frühsyrischer Theologie.   Münsterische Beiträge zur
Theologie 46. Münster: Aschendorff, 1979.

Cullmann, O. Early Christian Worship. Trans. A. Stewart Todd
and James B. Torrance. SBT 10. London: SCM, 1953.

Daniélou, Jean. The Theology of Jewish Christianity. Trans.
John A. Baker. Philadelphia: Westminster, 1964.

Dautzenberg, G. Urchristliche Prophetie: Ihre Erforschung,
ihre Voraussetzungen im Judentum und ihre Struktur im
ersten Korintherbrief. Stuttgart: Kohlhammer, 1975.

Delcor, M. "Le vocabulaire juridique, cultique et mystique de
l''initiation' dans la secte de Qumrân."   In Qumran-
Probleme.   Ed. H. Bardtke.   Berlin: Akademie-Verlag,
1963, 109-134.

_____. Rev. of The Odes of Solomon by J. H. Charlesworth.
BLE 76 (1975) 145ff.

Delling, Gerhard. "plērōma." TDNT 6 (1968) 298-305.

Denis, A. M. Rev. of The Odes of Solomon by J. H.
    Charlesworth. Muséon 88 (1975) 234ff.

Dibelius, Martin. Die Formgeschichte des Evangeliums.
    Tübingen: J. C. B. Mohr, 1933.

_____ and Hans Conzelmann. The Pastoral Epistles.
    Hermeneia. Trans. Philip Buttolph and Adela Yarbro.
    Philadelphia: Fortress, 1972.

Dodd, C. H. The Interpretation of the Fourth Gospel.
    Cambridge: University Press, 1955.

Drijvers, H. J. W. "Die Oden Salomos und die Polemik mit den
    Markioniten im syrischen Christentum." In Symposium
    Syriacum 1976. Orientalia Christiana Analecta 205.
    Rome: Oriental Institute, 1978, 39-55.

_____. "Edessa und das jüdische Christentum." VC 24
    (1970) 4-33.

_____. "Facts and Problems in Early Syriac-Speaking
    Christianity." The Second Century 2 (1982) 157-175.

_____. "Kerygma und Logos in den Oden Salomos dargestellt
    am Beispiel der 23. Ode." In Kerygma und Logos.
    Festschrift für C. Andresen. Ed. A. M. Ritter.
    Göttingen: Vandenhoeck & Ruprecht, 1979, 153-172.

_____. "Odes of Solomon and Psalms of Mani. Christians
    and Manichaeans in Third-Century Syria." In Studies in
    Gnosticism and Hellenistic Religions Presented to Gilles
    Quispel. Ed. R. van den Broek and M. J. Vermaseren.
    EPRO 91. Leiden: Brill, 1981, 117-130.

_____. "Rechtgläubigkeit und Ketzerei im ältesten
    syrischen Christentum." In Symposium Syriacum 1972.
    Orientalia Christiana Analecta 197. Rome: Oriental
    Institute, 1974, 291-308.

_____. "The 19th Ode of Solomon. Its Interpretation and
    Place in Syrian Christianity." JTS 31 (1980) 337-355.

_____. "The Origins of Gnosticism as a Religious and
    Historical Problem." NedTTs 22 (1968) 321-351.

Driver, G. R. "Notes on Two Passages in the Odes of Solomon."
    JTS 25 (1974) 434-439.

Ellis, E. Earle. Prophecy and Hermeneutics in Early
    Christianity. New Testament Essays. WUNT 18. Tübingen:
    J. C. B. Mohr, 1978.

Emerton, J. A. and R. P. Gorden. "A Problem in the Odes of
    Solomon XXIII.20." JTS 32 (1981) 443-447.

_____. "Notes on Some Passages in the Odes of Solomon."
JTS 28 (1977) 507-519.

_____. "Some Problems of Text and Language in the Odes of
Solomon." JTS 18 (1967) 372-406.

Erbetta, Mario. Gli Apocrifi del Nuovo Testamento I/1.
Vangeli. Torino, Roma: Marietti, 1975.

Evans, Craig A. "Current Issues in Coptic Gnosticism for New
Testament Study." Studia Biblica et Theologica 9 (1979)
109-113.

Fanourgakis, Vassilios. Hai Ōdai Solomōntos; Symbolē eis tēn
ereunan tēs hymnographias tēs Archaikēs Ekklēsias.
Analecta Vlatadon 29. Thessalonikii: Patriarchal
Institute for Patristic Studies, 1979.

Filoramo, G. "Pneuma e luce in alcuni testi gnostici."
Augustinianum 20 (1980) 595-614.

Fitzmyer, Joseph A. A Wandering Aramean. Collected Aramaic
Essays. SBLMS 25. Missoula: Scholars, 1979.

_____. "Nouveau Testament et Christologie: Questions
actuelles." NRT 103 (1981) 18-47; 187-221.

Fohrer, Georg. History of Israelite Religion. Trans. David
E. Green. Nashville: Abingdon, 1972.

_____. Rev. of The Odes of Solomon, by J. H. Charlesworth.
ZAW 86 (1974) 117.

Frankenberg, W. Das Verständnis der Oden Salomos. BZAW 21.
Giessen: Töpelmann, 1911.

Fries, S. A. "Die Oden Salomos. Montanistische Lieder aus
dem 2. Jahrhundert." ZNW 12 (1911) 108-125.

Fuller, Reginald H. The Foundations of New Testament
Christology. New York: Charles Scribner's Sons, 1965.

Gamber, K. "Die Oden Salomos als frühchristliche Gesänge beim
heiligen Mahl." Ostkirchliche Studien 15 (1966) 182-195.

Georgi, Dieter. "Der vorpaulinische Hymnus Phil 2, 6-11." In
Zeit und Geschichte. Dankesgabe an Rudolf Bultmann zum
80. Geburtstag. Ed. Erich Dinkler. Tübingen: J. C. B.
Mohr, 1964, 263-293.

_____. Weisheit Salomos. Gütersloh: Gerd Mohn, 1979.

Gero, Stephan. "The Spirit as a Dove at the Baptism of
Jesus." NovT 18 (1976) 17-35.

Gerstenberger, E. "Psalms." In Old Testament Form Criticism.
    Ed. John H. Hayes. San Antonio: Trinity University,
    1974, 180-220.

Gibson, J. C. L. "From Qumran to Edessa or the Aramaic
    Speaking Church Before and After 70 A.D." ALUOS 5 (1966)
    24-39.

Goppelt, Leonhard. Der Erste Petrusbrief. MeyerK 12.1.
    Göttingen: Vandenhoeck & Ruprecht, 1978.

Graffin, G. "Recherches sur le thème de l'Eglise-Epouse dan
    les liturgies et la littérature patristique de langue
    syriaque." OrSyr 3 (1958) 317-336.

Grant, R. M. "The Odes of Solomon and the Church of Antioch."
    JBL 63 (1944) 363-377.

Gressmann, H. "Die Oden Salomos." In Neutestamentliche
    Apokryphen. Zweite Auflage. Ed. E. Hennecke. Tübingen:
    J. C. B. Mohr, 1924, 437-472.

Grillmeier, A. "Der Gottessohn im Totenreich." ZKT 71 (1949)
    1-53, 184-203.

_____. "Höllenabstieg." ZTK 5 (1960) 450-455.

Grimme, H. Die Oden Salomos: Syrisch-Hebräisch-Deutsch.
    Heidelberg: Carl Winters Universitätsverlag, 1911.

Grönzinger, Karl-Erich. "Singen und ekstatische Sprache in
    der frühen jüdischen Mystik." JSJ 11 (1980) 66-77.

Gruenwald, Ithamar. Apocalyptic and Merkavah Mysticism. AGJU
    14. Leiden: Brill, 1980.

_____. "Knowledge and Vision: Towards a Classification of
    the Two "Gnostic" Concepts in the Light of their Alleged
    Origins." Israel Oriental Studies 3 (1973) 63-107.

_____. "The Jewish Esoteric Literature in the Time of the
    Mishnah and Talmud." Immanuel 4 (1974) 37-46.

Grundmann, Walter. "tapeinos." TDNT 8 (1972) 1-26.

Guirau, J. and A. G. Hamman. Les Odes de Salomon. Paris:
    Desclée de Brouwer, 1981.

Gunkel, Herrmann. "Die Oden Salomos." In Reden und Aufsätze.
    Göttingen: Vandenhoeck & Ruprecht, 1913, 163-192.

_____. "Die Oden Salomos." ZNW 11 (1910) 291-328.

_____. Die Wirkung des Heiligen Geistes. Göttingen:
    Vandenhoeck & Ruprecht, 1909.

_____. Einleitung in die Psalmen. 2nd Ed. Göttingen:
Vandenhoeck & Ruprecht, 1933.

Hahn, Ferdinand. The Titles of Jesus in Christology. Trans.
Harold Knight and George Ogg. New York and Cleveland:
Word, 1963.

_____. The Worship of the Early Church. Trans. David E.
Green. Philadelphia: Fortress, 1973.

Hammerton-Kelly, R. G. Pre-Existence, Wisdom and the Son of
Man. SNTSMS 21. Cambridge: University Press, 1973.

Harder, Gunther. "phtheirō." TDNT 9 (1974) 93-106.

Harnack, A. and J. Flemming. Ein jüdisch-christliches
Psalmbuch aus dem ersten Jahrhundert. TU 35. Leipzig:
Hinrichs'sche Buchhandlung, 1910.

Harrington, Daniel J. Rev. of The Odes of Solomon, by J. H.
Charlesworth. CBQ 37 (1975) 104ff.

Harris, J. R. and A. Mingana. The Odes and Psalms of Solomon.
2 vols. Manchester: University Press, 1916 and 1920.

Hausschild, W. D. Gottes Geist und der Mensch. Studien zur
frühchristlichen Pneumatologie. BEvT 63. Munchen: C.
Kaiser 1972.

Heidland, Wolfgang. "oxos." TDNT 5 (1967) 288-289.

Hengel, Martin. "Hymnus und Christologie." In Wort in der
Zeit. Festgabe für Karl Heinrich Rengstorf. Ed. W.
Haubeck and H. Bachmann. Leiden: Brill, 1980, 1-21.

_____. The Son of God. The Origin of Christology and the
History of Jewish-Hellenistic Religion. Trans. John
Bowden. Philadelphia: Fortress, 1976.

Hill, David. New Testament Prophecy. Atlanta: John Knox,
1979.

Holm-Nielsen, Svend. "'Ich' in den Hodajoth und die Qumrangemeinde." In Qumran-Probleme. Ed. H. Bardtke. Berlin:
Akademie-Verlag, 1963, 217-229.

_____. "Religiöse Poesie des Spätjudentum." Aufstieg und
Niedergang der römischen Welt 19.1 (1979) 152-186.

Hora, E. "Die Oden Salomos." TG 5 (1913) 128-140.

Horsely, R. A. "Spiritual Marriage with Sophia." VC 33
(1979) 30-54.

Jansen, H. Ludin. Die spätjüdische Psalmdichtung. Ihr
    Entstehungskreis und ihr "Sitz im Leben." Oslo: Jacob
    Dybwad, 1937.

Jeremias, Joachim. "abyssos." TDNT 1 (1964) 9-10.

_____. Die Briefe an Timotheus und Titus. NTD 9.
    Göttingen: Vandenhoeck & Ruprecht, 1963.

Jeremias, Jörg. Theophanie: die Geschichte einer alttesta-
    mentlicher Gattung. WMANT 10. Neukirchen: Vluyn, 1965.

Jonas, Hans. "Myth and Mysticism." JR 49 (1969) 315-329.

_____. The Gnostic Religion. Boston: Beacon, 1963.

Käsemann, E. Das wandernde Gottesvolk: Eine Untersuchung zum
    Hebräerbrief. FRLANT 55. Göttingen: Vandenhoeck &
    Ruprecht, 1957.

Keck, Leander E. A Future for the Historical Jesus.
    Philadelphia: Fortress, 1980.

Kittel, Gerhard. Die Oden Salomos: Überarbeitet oder
    einheitlich? Beiträge zur Wissenschaft vom Alten Testa-
    ment 16. Leipzig: J. C. Hinrichs'sche Buchhandlung,
    1914.

_____. "Eine zweite Handschrift der Oden Salomos." ZNW 14
    (1913) 79-93.

Klijn, A. F. J. Rev. of Die Oden Salomos, by Michael Lattke.
    VC 34 (1980) 302-304.

Köbert, R. "Oden Salomos 20, 6 und Sir. 33, 31." Bib 58
    (1977) 529-530.

_____. Rev. of Die Oden Salomos, by Michael Lattke. Bib
    61 (1980) 433-434.

Koester, Helmut. Introduction to the New Testament. 2 vols.
    Philadelphia: Fortress, 1982.

_____. Rev. of Weisheit und Torheit, by Ulrich Wilckens.
    Gnomon 33 (1961) 591-595.

_____ and James A. Robinson. Trajectories through Early
    Christianity. Philadelphia: Fortress, 1971.

Kowalski, A. "'Rivestiti di gloria' Adamo ed Eva nel commento
    di S. Efrem a Gen 2,25 (Ricerca sulle fonti dell'esegesi
    siriaca)." Cristianesimo nella Storia 3 (1982) 41-60.

Kraus, Hans Joachim. Psalmen. 2 vols. BKAT 15. Neukirchen:
    Neukirchener Verlag, 1960.

Kroll, Josef. Die christliche Hymnodik bis zu Klemens von Alexandreia. Verzeichnis der Vorlesungen an der Akademie zu Braunsberg, Sommer-Semester. Königsberg: Hartungsche Buchdruckerei, 1921.

Küchler, Max. Frühjüdische Weisheitstraditionen. Zum Fortgang weisheitlichen Denkens im Bereich des frühjüd-ischen Jahweglaubens. OBO 26. Freiburg: Universitäts-verlag, 1979.

Kuhn, H.-W. Enderwartung und gegenwärtiges Heil. SUNT 4. Göttingen: Vandenhoeck & Ruprecht, 1966.

Labourt, J. and P. Batiffol. Les Odes de Salomon: une oeuvre chrétienne des environs de l'an 100-120. Paris: Librairie Lecoffre, 1936.

La Fargue, John Michael. Language and Gnosis: Form and Meaning in the Acts of Thomas ch 1-10. Th.D. Diss.; Harvard Divinity School, 1977.

Lagrand, James. "How Was the Virgin Mary 'Like a Man'?" NT 22 (1980) 97-107.

Langbrantner, Wolfgang. Weltferner Gott oder Gott der Liebe. Der Ketzerstreit in der johanneischen Kirche. Beiträge zur biblischen Exegese und Theologie 6. Frankfurt: Peter Lang, 1977.

Lattke, Michael. Die Oden Salomos in ihrer Bedeutung für Neues Testament und Gnosis. 3 vols. OBO 25/1-3. Göttingen: Vandenhoeck & Ruprecht, 1979, 1980.

_____. Einheit im Wort. Die spezifische Bedeutung von "agapē," "agapan," und "philein" im Johannesevangelium. SANT 41. München: Kösel, 1975.

_____. "The Odes of Solomon in Pistis Sophia. An Example of Gnostic "exegesis"." East Asia Journal of Theology 1 (1983) 58-69.

Le Déaut, Roger. "Le thème de la circoncision du coeur." Congress Volume, Vienna, 1980. VTSup 32. Leiden: Brill, 1981, 178-205.

Lindblom, Johannes. Om lifvetz idé hos Paulus och Johannes samt i de s.k. Salomos oden. Uppsala Universitets Årsskrift 1910: Teologi 1. Uppsala: Akademiska boktryckeriet E. Berling, 1911.

Lohse, Edward. "cheir." TDNT 9 (1974) 424-434.

_____. Colossians and Philemon. Hermeneia. Trans. William Poehlmann and Robert J. Karris. Philadelphia: Fortress, 1973.

Luzzaraga, J. Las Tradiciones de la Nube en la Biblia y en
     Judaismo Primitivo. AnBib 54. Rome: Biblical Insti-
     tute, 1973.

Maas, W. Gott und die Hölle. Studien zum Descensus Christi.
     Einsiedeln: Johannes-Verlag, 1979.

Mack, Burton L. Logos und Sophia: Untersuchungen zur
     Weisheitstheologie   im   hellenistischen   Judentum.
     Göttingen: Vandenhoeck & Ruprecht, 1973.

Macomber, W. F. Rev. of The Odes of Solomon, by J. H.
     Charlesworth. Orientalia Christiana Periodica 40 (1974)
     437ff.

MacRae, George W. "The Jewish Background of the Gnostic
     Sophia Myth." NT 12 (1970) 86-101.

McKenzie, J. L. "Darkness." Dictionary of the Bible.
     Milwaukee: Bruce, 1965, 175.

McNeil, Brian. "A Liturgical Source in Acts of Peter 38."
     VC 33 (1979) 342-346.

_____. "Le Christ en vérité est Un." Irénikon 51 (1978)
     198-202.

_____. Rev. of Die Oden Salomos, by Michael Lattke.
     Ostkirchliche Studien 29 (1980) 193-194.

_____. "The Odes of Solomon and the Sufferings of Christ."
     In Symposium Syriacum 1976. Orientalia Christiana
     Analecta 205. Rome: Oriental Institute, 1978, 31-38.

Merrill, E. H. "The Odes of Solomon and the Acts of Thomas:
     A Comparative Study." Journal of the Evangelical Theol-
     ogy Society 17 (1974) 231-234.

Michel, Otto. "Spätjüdisches Prophetentum." In Neutestament-
     liche Studien für Rudolf Bultmann. Ed. W. Eltester.
     Berlin: Töpelmann, 1957, 60-66.

Moule, C. F. D. The Epistle to the Colossians and to
     Philemon. Cambridge: University Press, 1958.

_____. The Holy Spirit. London and Oxford: Mowbrays,
     1978.

_____. The Origin of Christology. New York: Cambridge
     University, 1977.

Müller, U. B. Prophetie und Predigt im Neuen Testament;
     Formgeschichtliche Untersuchungen zur urchristlichen
     Prophetie. Gütersloh: Gerd Mohn, 1975.

Murray, Robert. "Recent Studies in Early Symbolic Theology."
     HeyJ 6 (1965) 412-433.

Murray, Robert. Symbols of Church and Kingdom. A Study in
    Early Syriac Tradition. London: Cambridge University,
    1975.

_____. "The Exhortation to Candidates for Ascetical Vows
    at Baptism in the Ancient Syriac Church." NTS 21 (1974-
    75) 59-80.

Mussner, Franz. Christus das All und die Kirche. Trier:
    Paulinus, 1968.

Nickelsburg, George W. E. Jewish Literature Between the Bible
    and the Mishnah. Philadelphia: Fortress, 1981.

_____. Resurrection, Immortality, and Eternal Life in
    Intertestamental Judaism. HTS 26. Cambridge: Harvard,
    1972.

Nock, Arthur Darby. Early Gentile Christianity and its
    Hellenistic Background. New York: Harper, 1964.

Norden, Eduard. Agnostos Theos. Untersuchungen zur Formge-
    schichte religiöser Rede. Darmstadt: Wissenschaftliche
    Buchgesellschaft, 1956.

Odeberg, H. "Foreställoringarṇa om Metatron i äldre judisk
    mystik." Krykohistorisk Årsskrift 27 (1927) 1-20.

Orbe, A. La Theología del Espiritu Santo: Estudios
    Valentinos IV. Rome: Gregorian, 1966.

Panagopoulos, J. Prophetic Vocation in the New Testament and
    Today. Leiden: Brill, 1977.

Peel, Malcolm L. "The 'Descensus Ad Inferos' in 'The Teach-
    ings of Silvanus' (CG VII, 4)." Numen 26 (1982) 23-49.

Peterson, Erich. The Angels and the Liturgy. London:
    Darton, Longman and Todd, 1964.

Petzke, G. Die Tradition von Apollonius von Tyana und das
    Neue Testament. Leiden: Brill, 1970.

Philonenko, Marc. "Conjecture sur un verset de la onzième Ode
    de Salomon." ZNW 53 (1962) 264.

_____. Joseph et Aséneth. Introduction, texte critique,
    traduction et notes. Leiden: Brill, 1968.

Quell, Gottfried. "eklegomai." TDNT 4 (1967) 145-168.

Reiling, Jannes. Hermas and Christian Prophecy. Leiden:
    Brill, 1973.

Reinink, G. J. Rev. of The Odes of Solomon, by J. H.
    Charlesworth. JSJ 5 (1974) 64-68.

Robertson, D. "Literature, The Bible as." IDBSup, New York:
    Abington, 1976, 547-551.

Robinson, James M. "Die Hodajot-Formel im Gebet und Hymnus
    des Frühchristentums." In Apophoreta. Festschrift für
    Ernst Haenchen. Ed. W. Eltester and F. W. Kettler.
    Berlin: Töpelmann, 1964, 194-235.

Rowland, C. "The Visions of God in Apocalyptic Literature."
    JSJ 10 (1979) 37-154.

Rudolf, Kurt. Die Gnosis: Wesen und Geschichte einer spät-
    antiken Religion. Göttingen: Vandenhoeck & Ruprecht,
    1978.

_____. "Perlenlied und Oden Salomos." TRu 34 (1969)
    214-224.

_____. "War der Verfasser der Oden Salomos ein 'Qumran-
    Christ?" RevQ 4 (1964) 523-555.

Sanders, Jack T. The New Testament Christological Hymns.
    Their Historical Religious Background. SNTSMS 15.
    Cambridge: University Press, 1971.

Sasse, Hermann. "aiōn." TDNT 2 (1964) 197-209.

Schäfer, P. Die Vorstellung vom Heiligen Geist in der
    rabbinischen Literatur. SANT 28. München: Kösel, 1972.

_____. Rivalität zwischen Englen und Menschen. Berlin:
    de Gruyter, 1975.

Schenke, Hans-Martin. Die Herkunft der sogenannten Evangelium
    Veritatis. Göttingen: Vandenhoeck & Ruprecht, 1959.

_____. "Die Tendenz der Weisheit zur Gnosis." In Gnosis.
    Festschrift für Hans Jonas. Ed. Barbara Aland.
    Göttingen: Vandenhoeck & Ruprecht, 1978, 361-364.

Schille, G. Frühchristliche Hymnen. Berlin: Evangelische
    Verlagsanstalt, 1965.

Schlier, Henrich. Christus und die Kirche im Epheserbrief.
    BHT 6. Tübingen: Vandenhoeck & Ruprecht, 1930.

_____. "gala." TDNT 1 (1964) 647.

Schmithals, Walter. Die Gnosis in Korinth. FRLANT 66.
    Göttingen: Vandenhoeck & Ruprecht, 1956.

Scholem, Gershom. Jewish Gnosticism, Merkabah Mysticism, and
    Talmudic Tradition. 2nd Ed. New York: Jewish Theolog-
    ical Seminary of America, 1965.

_____. Major Trends in Jewish Mysticism. New York: Schocken, 1954.

_____. On the Kabbalah and its Symbolism. New York: Schocken, 1965.

Schrenk, Gottlob. "eklektos." TDNT 4 (1967) 186-192.

Schüpphaus, Joachim. Die Psalmen Salomos. ALGHJ 7. Leiden: Brill, 1979.

Schüssler, Fiorenza, Elizabeth. "Wisdom Mythology and Christological Hymns of the New Testament." In Aspects of Wisdom in Judaism and Early Christianity. Ed. Robert L. Wilken. Notre Dame: University of Notre Dame, 1975, 18-38.

Schulthess, F. "Textkritische Bemerkungen zu den syrischen Oden Salomos." ZNW 11 (1910) 249-257.

Schwartz, Jacques. "Le voyage au ciel dans la littérature apocalyptique." In L'Apocalyptique. Etudes D'Histoire Des Religions 3. Paris: Librairie Orientaliste Paul Geuthner, 1977, 91-126.

Schweizer, Eduard. "hyios." TDNT 8 (1972) 387-392.

Scott, R. B. Y. Proverbs. AB 18. Garden City: Doubleday, 1956.

Seesemann, Heinrich. "pateō." TDNT 5 (1967) 940-945.

Segelberg, Eric. Masbūtā. Studies in the Ritual of the Mandaean Baptism. Uppsala: Bokryckerei Aktiebolag, 1958.

_____. "The Baptismal Rite According to Some of the Coptic Gnostic Texts of Nag Hammadi." Studia Patristica 80 (1962) 117-128.

Sjöberg, E. "Neuschöpfung in den Toten-Meer Rollen." ST 9 (1956) 131-136.

_____. "Wiedergeburt und Neuschöpfung im palästinischen Judentum." ST 4 (1951) 44-85.

Slee, H. M. "A Note on the Sixteenth Ode of Solomon." JTS 15 (1914) 454.

Smith, Jonathan Z. "The Prayer of Joseph." In Religions in Antiquity. Essays in Memory of E. R. Goodenough. Supplments to Numen 14. Ed. Jacob Neusner. Leiden: Brill, 1968, 142-160.

Southwell, P. J. M. Rev. of The Odes of Solomon, by J. H. Charlesworth. JTS 25 (1974) 506-508.

Spitta, F. "Zum Verständnis der Oden Salomos." ZNW 11 (1910) 193-203.

Strugnell, John. "The Angelic Liturgy at Qumran - 4Q Serek šîrôt ôlat haššabbāt." Congress Volume. VTSup 7. Leiden: Brill, 1960, 318-345.

Talbert, Charles H. "The Myth of a Descending-Ascending Redeemer in Mediterranean Antiquity." NTS 22 (1976) 418-439.

Terzoli, Riccardo. Il Tema della Beatitudine nei Padri Siri. Brescia: Morcelliana, 1972.

_____. "Repertorio dei nomi divine nelle Odi di Salomone." Vetera Christianorum 11 1974) 125-140.

Testuz, M. Papyrus Bodmer VII IX. Cologne-Geneva: Bibliotheque Bodmer, 1959.

Tosato, A. "Gesù e gli zeloti alla luce delle Ode di Salomoni." BibOr 19 (1977) 145-153.

_____. "Il battesimo di Gesù e le Odi di Salomone." BibOr 18 (1976) 261-269.

Tsakonas, V. G. "Hai Ōdai Solomōntos. Eisagōgē - Keimenon - Hermeneia." Theologia 44 (1973) 389-416; 45 (1974) 129-149, 309-346, 511-558, 608-646.

Turner, J. D. "The Gnostic Threefold Path to Enlightenment." NT 22 (1980) 324-351.

Ungnad, A. and W. Staerk. Die Oden Salomos: Aus dem Syrischen übersetzt, mit Anmerkungen. KlT 64. Bonn: A. Markus und E. Weber, 1910.

Vajda, G. "Jewish Mysticism." Encyclopaedia Britannica 10 (1974) 184-185.

Van Overstraeten, Jeanne-Ghislaine. "Les liturgies nuptiales des églises de langue syriaque et le mystère de l'Eglise-Epouse." Parole De L'Orient 8 (1977) 235-311.

Vielhauer, P. "'Anapausis' Zum gnostischen Hintergrund des Thomas-Evangeliums." In Apophoreta. Festschrift für Ernst Haenchen. Ed. W. Eltester, F. H. Kettler. Berlin: Töpelmann, 1964, 281-299.

Vööbus, A. "Neues Licht zur Frage der Originalsprache der Oden Salomos." Muséon 75 (1962) 275-290.

Vogels, H. J. Christi Abstieg ins Totenreich und das Läuterungsgericht an den Toten. Eine bibeltheologisch-dogmatische Untersuchung zum Glaubensartikel "descendit ad inferos." Freiburger Theologische Studien 102. Freiburg: Herder, 1976.

Vogl, August. "Oden Salomos 17, 22, 24, 42." Ed. Brian
    McNeil. OrChr 62 (1978) 60-73.

Volz, Paul. Die Eschatologie der jüdischen Gemeinde im
    neutestamentlichen Zeitalter. Tübingen: J. C. B. Mohr,
    1934.

von Rad, Gerhard. "eirēnē." TDNT 2 (1964) 402-406.

_____. Wisdom in Israel. Nashville: Abingdon, 1972.

Weiss, Hans-Friedrich. Untersuchungen zur Kosmologie des
    hellenistischen und palästinischen Judentum. TU 97.
    Berlin: Akademie-Verlag, 1966.

Wickham, L. R. Rev. of The Odes of Solomon, by J. H.
    Charlesworth. JSS 20 (1975) 122ff.

Widengren, Geo. "Baptism and Enthronement in Some Jewish-
    Christian Documents." In The Saviour God: Comparative
    Studies in the Concept of Salvation Presented to Edwin
    Oliver James. Ed. S. G. F. Brandon. Manchester:
    University of Manchester, 1963, 205-217.

_____. "Den himmelska intronisation och dopet." Religion
    och Bibel. Nathan Söderblom-Sällskapets Årsbok 5.
    Stockholm: Svenska. Kyrkans Diakonistyrelses Bokförlag,
    1946, 28-61.

_____. "Heavenly Enthronement and Baptism. Studies in
    Mandaean Baptism." In Religions in Antiquity. Essays in
    Memory of E. R. Goodenough. Supplement to Numen 14. Ed.
    Jacob Neusner. Leiden: Brill, 1968, 551-582.

_____. Mesopotamian Elements in Manichaeism. Uppsala:
    Lundequistska Bokhandeln, 1946.

_____. "Réflexions sur le baptême dans la chrétienté
    syriaque. In Paganisme, Judaisme, Christianisme.
    Mélanges offerts à Marcel Simon. Ed. A. Benoit, M.
    Philonenko. Paris: Editions E. DeBoccard, 1978,
    347-357.

_____. The Ascension of the Apostle and the Heavenly Book.
    Uppsala: Lundequistska Bokhandeln, 1950.

Wilckens, Ulrich. "sophia." TDNT 7 (1971) 507-509.

_____. Weisheit und Torheit. Eine exegetisch-
    religionsgeschichtliche Untersuchung zu 1 Kor. 1 und 2.
    BHT 26. Tübingen: J. C. B. John, 1959.

Windisch, Hans. Der zweite Korintherbrief. MeyK Abt 6. Ed.
    George Strecker. Göttingen: Vandenhoeck & Ruprecht, 1970.

Winkler, Gabriele. "The Original Meaning of the Prebaptismal
    Anointing and Its Implications." Worship 52 (1978)
    24-44.

_____. "Zu frühchristlichen Tauftradition in Syrien und Armenien unter Einbezug der Taufe Jesu." Ostkirchliche Studien 27 (1978) 281-306.

Winston, David. The Wisdom of Solomon. AB 43. Garden City: Doubleday, 1979.

Worrell, W. H. "The Odes of Solomon and the Pistis Sophia." JTS 13 (1911) 29-46.

Yamauchi, Edwin. Pre-Christian Gnosticism. Grand Rapids: Eerdmanns, 1973.

_____. "Pre-Christian Gnosticism in the Nag Hammadi Texts?" CH 48 (1979) 129-141.

Young, Frances. "Two Roots or a Tangled Mass?" In The Myth of God Incarnate. Ed. John Hick. Philadelphia: Westminster, 1977, 88-93.

ABBREVIATIONS

Abbreviations used in the text, the notes and the bibliography for biblical books, pseudepigraphical and early Patristic works, for Dead Sea Scrolls and Nag Hammadi Tractates, for periodicals, reference works and serials conform to the system of abbreviations set forth in "Instructions for Contributors," Journal of Biblical Literature 95 (1976).

Reference Works and Works Frequently Cited

Bauer
    W. Bauer, Die Oden Salomos (Kleine Texte 64; Berlin: de Gruyter, 1933).

Bernard
    J. H. Bernard, The Odes of Solomon (Texts and Studies 8.3; Cambridge: University, 1912).

Beskow and Hidal
    P. Beskow and S. Hidal, Salomos Oden. Den äldsta kristna Sångboken översatt och kommenterad (Stockholm: Proprius, 1980).

Brockelmann
    K. Brockelmann, Lexicon Syriacum (Hildesheim: Georg Olms, 1966).

Bruston
    C. Bruston, Les plus anciens cantiques chrétiens (Paris:
    Librairie Fischbacher, 1912).

Charlesworth
    J. H. Charlesworth, The Odes of Solomon (SBLTT 13;
    Missoula: Scholars, 1977).

Crum
    W. E. Crum, A Coptic Dictionary (Oxford: Clarendon,
    1939).

Erbetta
    M. Erbetta, Gli Apocrifi del Nuovo Testamento I/1.
    Vangeli (Torino, Roma: Marietti, 1975).

Harnack and Flemming
    A. Harnack and J. Flemming, Ein jüdisch-christliches
    Psalmbuch (TU 35; Leipzig: Hinrichs'sche Buchhandlung,
    1910).

Harris and Mingana
    J. R. Harris and A. Mingana, The Odes and Psalms of
    Solomon (2 vols.; Manchester: University Press, 1916 and
    1920).

Labourt and Batiffol
    J. Labourt and P. Batiffol, Les Odes de Salomon: une
    oeuvre chrétienne des environs de l'an 100-120 (Paris:
    Librairie Lecoffre, 1936).

Lattke
    M. Lattke, Die Oden Salomos in ihrer Bedeutung für Neues
    Testament und Gnosis (3 vols.; OBO 25/1-3; Göttingen:
    Vandenhoeck & Ruprecht, 1979, 1980).

Nöldeke
    T. Nöldeke, Kurzgefasste syrische Grammatik (Darmstadt:
    Wissenschaftliche Buchgesellschaft, 1966).

Payne Smith
    J. Payne Smith (ed.) A Compendious Syriac Dictionary
    (Oxford: Clarendon Press, 1903).

Tsakonas
    V. G. Tsakonas, "Hai Ōdai Solomōntos. Eisagōgē-Keimenon-
    Hermeneia," Theologia 44 (1973) 389-416; 45 (1974) 129-
    149, 309-346, 511-558, 608-646.

Ungnad and Staerk
    A. Ungnad and W. Staerk, Die Oden Salomos: Aus dem
    Syrischen übersetzt, mit Anmerkungen. (Kleine Texte 64;
    Bonn: Markus & Weber, 1910).